THE MIRACLE
OF
BIBLICAL
INSPIRATION

A Refutation of:
Perfection of Translations (Idealism),
Derivative Inspiration, Double Inspiration,
Thought or Message Inspiration,
Partial Inspiration, Natural Inspiration,
Neoorthodox Inspiration, Inspiration of Men

by
H. D. Williams, M.D., Ph.D.

THE OLD PATHS PUBLICATIONS, Inc.
142 Gold Flume Way
Cleveland, Georgia, U.S.A.

BIBLE FOR TODAY #3392

Disclaimer

The author of this work has quoted the writers of many articles and books. This does not mean that the author endorses or recommends the works of others. If the author quotes someone, it does not mean that he agrees with all of the author's tenets, statements, concepts, or words, whether in the work quoted or any other work of the author. There has been no attempt to alter the meaning of the quotes; and therefore, some of the quotes are long in order to give the entire sense of the passage.

Copyright © 2009 by H. D. Williams
All Rights Reserved
Printed in the United States of America

Library of Congress Control Number: 2009920265
REL006100: Religion: Biblical Criticism & Interpretation

ISBN 978-0-9985452-6-4

All Scripture quotes are from the King James Bible except those verses compared and then the source is identified.

Address All Inquiries To:
THE OLD PATHS PUBLICATIONS, Inc.
142 Gold Flume Way
Cleveland, Georgia, U.S.A.

Web: www.theoldpathspublications.com
E-mail: TOP@theoldpathspublications.com

BIBLE FOR TODAY #3392
Web: www.biblefortoday.org
E-mail: bft@biblefortoday.org

1.0

"The more you study the Book, the more you will feel convinced that its many authors all resorted to one and the same Fountain of Inspiration." (from *Inspiration and Interpretation* by Dean John William Burgon, p. 175)

DEDICATION

This work is dedicated to all: (1) who are seeking the Scripture's declarations concerning the absolute and foundational authoritative Truth *"once delivered,"* (2) who crave to fulfill the Lord Jesus Christ's command, *"If you love me keep my commandments,"* and (3) who are looking for His *"glorious appearing."*

> *"Looking for that blessed hope, and the glorious appearing of the great God and our Saviour Jesus Christ;" Titus 2:13*

"THE THEOLOGICAL use of the term *inspiration* is a reference to that controlling influence which God exerted over the human authors by whom the Old and New Testaments were written. It has to do with the reception of the divine message and the accuracy with which it is transcribed...Without doubt it is the SUPERNATURAL element, which constitutes the very warp and woof of the Bible doctrine of inspiration..." (Lewis Sperry Chafer, *Systematic Theology Vol. 1 & 2* (Kregel Publications, Grand Rapids, MI, 1948, 1978 by Dallas Theological Seminary) p. 81. (HDW, my emphasis)

TABLE OF CONTENTS

Abbreviations

DE = dynamic equivalence translating, which is paraphrase translating for the receptor as opposed to the primary aim of FE translating of the <u>Words</u> of God for His glory.

e.g. = for example (L.)

FE = formal, verbal, plenary, equivalence translating

ff = following

FunE = functional equivalence translating, which is another name for dynamic equivalence translating.

i.e. = that is (L.)

KJB = King James Bible

MS = manuscript; a hand-written document on papyrus or vellum

MSS = manuscripts; hand-written documents on papyrus or vellum

NASB = New American Standard Bible

NIV = New International Version

NLT = New Living Translation

q.v. = which see (L.) in this work

TR/TT = Textus Receptus/Traditional Text

WCF = Westminster Confession of Faith

Definitions

1) **Autographs** = the original-language manuscripts (MSS) of the books of the Bible in Hebrew, Aramaic, and Greek that contain the Words that were given by *"inspiration of God"* and recorded by the Apostles and prophets as they were *"moved along"* by the Holy Spirit.

2) **Apographs** = manuscript copies of the autographs that may have unintentional scribal errors. It is obvious some MSS are purposefully corrupted. These MSS can not be called apographs.

3) **Equal** = the same, identical (word) (e.g. twelve = twelve).

4) **Equivalence** = corresponds, sameness (of a word). This is synonymous translating. For example, there may be 7 or 8 synonymous receptor-language words, but only one was chosen to translate an original-language Hebrew, Aramaic, or Greek Word because the word's "signification" in context reflects most closely the original (e.g. a dozen is equivalent to twelve). Equal implies exactly the same (word).

5) **Error** = mistake, blunder, inaccuracy, inexactness, confusion by disagreement of parts of Scripture; the antonym is accuracy.

6) **Formal** (translating) = a noun is translated for a noun, a verb for a verb, a pronoun for a pronoun, etc. so far as syntax of a language-group will allow.

7) **Inerrant** = simply **without error** or mistake, in contrast to infallible. We hesitate to use this strong word for the King James Bible because of various revisions over the years, although this author believes the translating of the King James Bible by the guidance of the Holy Spirit was without any translational errors.

But it had mistakes in printing, orthography, etc. (see below), which seems to be the plague of this author and others.

8) **Infallible** = **incapable of error.**

9) **Inspiration** = means **"God-breathed"** from the Greek word theopneustos (2 Tim. 3:16). It is a very technical Biblical term indicating a miraculous process and product. The Words of God originally given in Hebrew, Aramaic, and Greek to special men selected by God to record were "God-breathed." In this work, this is the **process** of inspiration. The **product** of inspiration in this work is the recorded inspired Words in Hebrew, Aramaic, and Greek in the sixty-sixty books of the canon of Scripture for man that are infallible and inerrant. "Inspiration" is a miracle. This means that God is the author of the original Words in Hebrew, Aramaic, and Greek, which is the Bible. The men who recorded them are not coauthors, although God used their vocabulary. This author believes that the Words that underlie the King James Bible English translation are the original perfect Words *"given by inspiration of God"* to *"holy men of God"* to record. God has providentially superintended the accurate, faithful, verbal, plenary, formal, equivalent translation of the Preserved[1] original-languages into the receptor-languages of the world so that some translations can be said to be without **translational** errors. In summary, *"**Inspiration** **is** (1) **the miracle** whereby **the Words** of*

---

[1] Dr. D. A. Waite's use of "Preserved" (with a capital) and "preserved" (not capitalized) has been adopted by many of us to designate the original Words with a capital and properly translated Words into a receptor language by a small "p." Therefore, we say: "The KJB is the Words of God preserved (small "p") in English." Or "The original Hebrew, Aramaic, and Greek Words are Preserved (capital "P")."

Scripture in Hebrew, Aramaic, and Greek were (2) **God-breathed** and **_"once delivered"_** using _"holy men of God"_ and their vocabulary, (3) who **recorded** them **"once"** perfectly as they were _"moved along"_ by the Holy Spirit (4) in such a way that **_"all"_** the Words written are **infallible and inerrant** in the sixty-six books of the canon of Scripture." A succinct way of stating the same thing is: **"The perfect author of the perfect Bible is God."**

10) **Idealism** = belief in perfection

11) **Perfection** or **perfect** = (IN THIS WORK) without sin, **incapable of error of any sort,** faultless, infallible, pure, without blemish, without spot, or without ANY contamination, and complete. In today's contentious atmosphere, this author believes that such **strong terms** as perfect and pure should only be applied theologically to God and His God-breathed Words. Otherwise, calling something "perfect" may cause someone to claim man or something produced by man is equal to the persons of the Trinity or His Words given by inspiration. This author is not talking about how the King James Bible translators did use the words "perfect" and "pure" in many places to signify completeness, maturity, or based upon the absolute pure or perfect. He is talking about:

(A) Our "perfect," sinless God; or the second person of the Trinity who only could act as the sinless _"perfect," "without blemish,"_ and _"without spot" "Lamb of God."_

(B) His miraculous Words, which were given _"once"_ to man by _"inspiration"_ as a "perfect" _"foundation"_ for ever.

   a)   In the King James Bible, perfect may mean _"without spot," "without blemish,"_ incapable of error, or sinless, as in Deut. 32:4, Psa. 18:30, James 1:17.

b)   In many other places, the context demands a sense of sinful man being complete, mature, or whole as in 2 Timothy 3:17, but retaining the capacity for sinning or of being influenced by sin (i.e. sinners). The Lord Jesus Christ was made "sin" but was not a sinner.

c)   In the writings of some authors, perfect often means complete or mature or based upon the proper textual source, but that is not the way perfect is used or defined in this work.

12) **Plenary** = **"all,"** complete, full, or not limited in any respect (i.e. plenary translating means all the Words were translated according to syntax).

13) **Preservation** = those precise Words received by "inspiration" are **Preserved** as promised by God because of His providential care. They are perfect as defined in this work because they are the same Words given to the Apostles and prophets to record (q.v.).

14) **Translations** vary depending on the method chosen to translate (e.g. verbal, formal equivalent (FE) **versus** dynamic equivalent (DE) or interpretive translating). The words chosen by man to translate the original 'received' inspired Words in the original languages of Hebrew, Aramaic, and Greek may be accurate, faithful, and without translational errors if they are translated by FE, but the words may not be perfect as defined in this work secondary to four reasons:

A)   **Printing mistakes;**

B)   **Orthographic mistakes;**

C)   **Synonym translating:** Synonyms chosen to translate an original-language word accurately and faithfully can be considered without translational error, but not so perfect that another word might **not** possibly be used (see equivalence above). One must be careful, however, with synonymous translating, which may or may not be accurate, because all synonyms do not carry the same "signification" or meaning. A translator could be guilty of semantics.[2] The King James Bible translators were superior skilled linguists, but they expressed the possibility that another word with the same "sense" (e.g. a synonym) might be possible to use in translating an inspired Word and even included some of them in the margin of the KJB.[3] In an accurate, faithful translation in any language, a synonym substitution or change could possibly be found to be better in future revisions. This is the reason for some revisions. This author does not know of ANY translation that has not undergone either a revision or another edition.[4]

D)   **The rules of grammar** when translating to properly express the meaning may vary from the original-language texts (Hebrew, Aramaic, or Greek) to the receptor-language (English, Spanish, etc.). For example, a participle may be translated as an imperative as in Mat. 28:20. This is in contrast to the original Words 'received' *"once"* because they were perfect in every sense, grammar included. God gave them perfectly the first time they were recorded as revelation by the

---

[2] H. D. Williams, M.D., Ph.D. et al, *Word-For-Word Translating, Verbal Plenary Translating* (The Old Paths Publications, Cleveland, GA, 2007) pp. 80, 98-100.

[3] Preface to the King James Bible, section, "Reasons Moving Us to Set Diversity in the Margin, Where There is a Great Probability of Each."

[4] Dr. Phil Stringer, *Ready Answers, A Response to the Evangelical and Fundamentalist Critics of the King James Bible* (Faith Baptist Church Publications, Ft. Pierce, FL) pp. 7-16. Also, see the information provided by Pastor Reagin in *The Lie That Changed the Modern World, A Refutation of the Modernist Cry, Poly-Scripturae* (Bible For Today Press, Collingswood, NJ, 2004, Also available on Amazon by title) p. 338ff.

Apostles and prophets to act as a *"foundation."* An accurate and faithful translation that is without **translational** errors may be called the Word of God in English, Spanish, French, Latin, etc., but it is not the inspired Word of God, which was *"once delivered"* perfectly by the miraculous process of "inspiration." A translation should not be referred to as inspired or given by inspiration because of the confusion it generates.

Lastly, before a translation is released to the public, those responsible for a translation should be as certain as possible that it is correct. It should not be subjected to constant or frequent manipulation through revisions or editions once released. This causes confusion comparable to the multiple modern texts and modern version fiasco. The properly translated KJB Words should never be changed for these reasons and in addition to the fact that it is an unparalleled English work of literature.

15) **Verbal** = **the words**. Therefore, verbal, plenary translating simply means "all the words."

CONTENDING FOR THE FAITH
By Henry M. Morris

"Beloved, when I gave all diligence to write unto you of the common salvation, it was needful for me to write unto you, and exhort you that ye should earnestly contend for **the faith which was once delivered unto the saints.**" (Jude 3) (HDW, my emphasis)

Jude long ago addressed a problem in his day which is still very real in our day among Christians. It is easier and more comfortable just to teach and preach about the blessings of our common salvation than it is to contend for the faith, but the latter is more "needful." The word conveys the idea that he was so constrained, evidently by the Holy Spirit, as actually to be in distress about this compelling need. Similarly, his exhortation to "earnestly contend" does not mean to "be argumentative," but rather, to "agonize with intense determination." It is one word in the Greek, epagonizomai (literally, "agonize over"). Defending and contending for the faith is serious, urgent business.

That which we are to defend is "the faith"--the whole body of Christian truth, wherever it is under attack. It would, of course, be especially important to contend for the doctrine of special creation, which is the foundation of all others, and which is the doctrine perpetually under the most concerted and persistent attack by the adversary.

That faith has been, long ago, "once delivered" to the saints. The sense of these words is "once for all turned over for safekeeping." The Lord has entrusted us with His Word, completed and inscripturated, and we must keep it, uncorrupted and intact, for every generation until He returns, preaching and teaching all of it to every creature, to the greatest extent we possibly can.

Finally, note that the safeguarding of the faith was not merely to specially trained theologians or other professionals, but to "the saints." Every Christian believer is commanded to "earnestly contend for the faith."

PREFACE

Keep Your Eye on the Ball

There is an old adage that most children are taught as they are growing up, related to playing a ballgame. As the ball is being thrown to the child, the parent warns him to: "Keep your eye on the ball!" The reason for this is obvious. If the child is not paying attention, he will miss the opportunity to catch or hit the ball. If competition is involved, the opponents often do things to distract the player, making him miss the ball. The entire game may be lost as a result. No successful ball player takes his eyes off the ball. Another way of saying this is that a successful player can not be distracted because he is focused on the ball.

This has application to today's battle over the "inspired" Words of God. The enemy is doing his best to distract the players on God's team. He would like nothing better than for believers to take their eyes off the Words that are *"given by inspiration of God."* Unfortunately, many are doing just that. Now that's taking your eye off the most important "ball" in your life.

There is One Ball

Just as most games have one ball (baseball, ping pong, basketball, football, soccer, tether ball, bowling, etc.) there is only **one** Scripture (Bible) *"given by inspiration of God."* *"Holy men of God spake as they were moved by the Holy Ghost"* to provide *"the faith **once delivered** unto the saints"* (2 Tim. 2:16, 2 Pe. 1:21, Jude 1:3).

Saints are on God's offensive team. Their quarterback is the Lord Jesus Christ. His cry is to *"Go ye therefore, and teach all nations, baptizing...teaching them to observe all things"* (Mat. 28:19-20). Now, that's a quarterback play-call or an offensive *"command."*

We can't teach *"all things"* properly if we take the wrong "ball" into the battle. We can't perform properly if we take a baseball into a football game or vice versa. We need the "ball" made by the process of perfection (*"inspiration"*). The perfect "ball" must be protected; it is the "ball" we must keep our eye upon.

Of course, the "ball" represents the original Words of the Bible in Hebrew, Aramaic, and Greek that were *"given by inspiration of God."* However, most of us need an accurate and faithful translation. This is like the following scenario in a football game. The coach of the team is God who gives the quarterback (the Lord Jesus Christ) the Words, usually in a code (language) that most do not understand, who in turn relates it to the team via the Holy Spirit. If the instructions are accurately and faithfully translated, understood, and executed, the Holy Spirit provides the power to propel the team to victory. Could the failure in our modern society be linked to the failure to handle the "ball" and translate the "code" properly? Has the authority of the Lord Jesus Christ and His Words temporarily lost the skirmish as a result?

All too often on the playing field, fights, arguments, accusations, false claims, and many other exhibitions of poor behavior occur. These distractions are the result of falling into the enemy's game plan and he would like nothing better than for the team to 'take their eyes off the ball.' Remember, the ball is the Words of God. It tells the story of the Redeemer from **one end to the other**. Do you remember the walk along the road to Emmaus in the Bible? Jesus walked with the couple to their home and along the way He revealed that the Scriptures from *"Moses and all the prophets"* were about Him (Lk 24:27)—**from one end to the other.**

The ball is the ***"foundation"*** of the game. Change the ball and you change the nature of the game. A game cannot be played with a defective ball or with the wrong ball. For example, we can't play football with a basketball. Similarly, change the Words in the Bible and the doctrine is changed and the "game of life" is no longer played by the *"rule"* (canon of Scripture).

Any ball game must be played with a precisely constructed ball and it is the same with the "game" of life. Life's "game ball" was constructed **one time** in a very precise way from a specific process that resulted in a special product. It was **a miracle** that only God could perform.

The Distraction

Have you ever noticed how coaches and ball players on the defensive team try to enlist the crowd to make "noise" when the offense has the ball? Well, the enemy is enlisting many good people to make lots of noise in the battle over *"inspiration"* of the Bible. Ultimately, it is designed to distract the offence, making them "take their eyes off the ball." Could all of this "noise" about *"inspiration"* today be designed by the enemy?

Many may think the issue of *"inspiration"* is a game or just a petty distraction, but it is much more. At the end of the matter is a product that is about the issue of eternal life—the inerrant, infallible, eternal Words of God given in Hebrew, Aramaic, and Greek because— *"So then faith cometh by hearing, and hearing by the word of God."* (Rom. 10:17). *"For by grace are ye saved by grace through faith..."* (Eph. 2:8). *"But without faith it is impossible to please him: for he that cometh to God must believe that he is, and that he is a rewarder of them that diligently seek him." (Hebrews 11:6).*

The original infallible, inerrant, Hebrew, Aramaic, and Greek Words is the "ball" that is the *"foundation"* of Christian life and faith, built on the *"rock,"* Jesus Christ (Lk. 6:48, 1 Cor. 3:11, Eph. 2:20). The Words that He gave us are a *"rock"* that will not *"pass away"* (Psa. 12:6-7, 119:89, 1 Pe. 1:23-25).

What are the most disconcerting things about all of the "noisy" attacks these days? There are two. **One** is the failure of many to understand that the **process** and **product** of *"inspiration"* is a "one time" miracle that can not and will not be repeated. **Second** is the failure of good men to recognize the enemy at work, trying to destroy the foundation from which accurate and faithful translations are made and by which *"all nations"* may be taught. All of this chatter about translations being inspired causes many to 'take their eye off the ball;' the Hebrew, Aramaic, and Greek Words *"given by inspiration of God."*

This author has written a work to follow that addresses some of these issues called *"The Miracle of Biblical Inspiration."* It is available through Bible For Today (BFT #3392) or on Amazon by typing in the title of the book (available February of 2009). It is an explanation of some important matters concerning *"inspiration"* with the hope that those who have "dropped the ball" will recover it, protect it, and carry it faithfully forward for the generations to come

May we all become united in this important matter. Amen!

H. D. Williams, M.D., Ph.D.

*"For David himself said by the Holy Ghost, The
LORD said to my Lord, Sit thou on my right hand,
till I make thine enemies thy footstool." Mark 12:36
"Which things also we speak, not in the words
which man's wisdom teacheth, but which the Holy
Ghost teacheth; comparing spiritual things with
spiritual." 1 Corinthians 2:13 (HDW, my emphasis)*

It is God's Bible

————"Hast thou ever heard
Of such a book? The author, God himself;
The subject, God and man, salvation, life
And death—eternal life, eternal death—
Dread words! whose meaning has no end, no bounds.
Most wondrous book! Bright candles of the Lord!
Star of eternity! The only star
By which the bark of man could navigate
The sea of life, and gain the coast of bliss
Securely! only star which rose on time,
And on its dark and troubled billows, stole,
As generations, drifting swiftly by,
Succeeded generation, thence a ray
Of heaven's own light, and to the hills of God,
Th' eternal hills, pointed the sinner's eye.
This book, this holy book, in every line
Marked with the seal of high divinity,
On every leaf bedewed with drops of love
Divine, and with the eternal heraldry
And signature of God Almighty stamped
From first to last—this ray of sacred light,
This lamp from off the everlasting throne,
Mercy took down, and in the night of time
Stood, casting on the dark her gracious bow,
And evermore beseeching men, with tears
And earnest sighs, to hear, believe, and live.
And many to her voice gave ear and read,
Believed, obeyed: and now, as the Amen,
True, faithful Witness swore, with snowy robes
And branching palms surround the fount of life,
And drink the streams of immortality,
Forever happy, and forever young."

(from the book by Gardiner Spring, D. D., *The Bible Not of Man, The Argument For the Divine Origin of the Sacred Scriptures, Drawn From the Scriptures Themselves* (American Tract Society, New York, NY, 1847) pp. 91-92.

CHAPTER 1

INTRODUCTION

The Purpose of This Work

The purpose of this brief work is to identify the various positions and relate them to which Words are *"given by inspiration of God"* or are "inspired." Many disagreements concerning the correct Biblical texts, translations, and *"inspiration"* of the Words can be traced to a misunderstanding of terms. Standardization of the terms must be sought. Confusion among those listening to pastors, evangelists, missionaries, and teachers results if God's saints are not in agreement about specific definitions, doctrines, and applications. God is not the author of confusion (1 Cor. 14:33). Therefore, we must define terms Biblically. Our Bibliology must be correct. Surely, most teachers understand that the Scripture defines important Words. *"Inspiration"* is defined in the Bible and men would benefit greatly if they would let the Scripture speak to them and not let other men determine their "belief."

The necessity to define words, especially when dealing with Biblical precepts, results from **(1)** differences in the meaning or signification of words in context in Scripture and **(2)** the divergence of opinions between those who are students of God's Words. The inattention to these aspects of linguistics has caused endless discussions among theologians, pastors, teachers, missionaries, evangelists, and translators. Often, it has prompted needless confusion and angst, particularly over the word, *"inspiration"* (theopneustos) and its use in context.

Furthermore, the books and articles about *"inspiration"* are almost limitless and opinions in the works vary GREATLY. The task at hand to evaluate the current discussion among religious leaders about *"inspiration"* is no small chore. Certain words are particularly sensitive. An attempt was made to keep this discussion short, but the author soon discovered that to be impossible.

CHAPTER 2

THE ATTEMPTS
TO EXPLAIN THE MIRACLE

The attempt by many men to explain the unexplainable process and product of *"inspiration,"* which is a miracle, has resulted in wide-ranging and often confusing opinions. For example, Dr. Charles Ryrie lists eight different definitions for *"inspiration."*[5] They are summarized here:

(1)   **Ryrie's definition:**
       "[B]iblical inspiration is that it is God's superintendence of the human authors so that, using their own individual personalities, they composed and recorded without error His revelation to man in the words of the original autographs. Several features of the definition are worth emphasizing: (1) God superintended but did not dictate the material. (2) He used human authors and their own individual styles. (3) Nevertheless, the product was, in its original manuscripts, without error.

(2)   **Natural Inspiration:**
       "...the "writers of the Bible were men of great genius, but that their writings were inspired no more than those of other geniuses throughout history."

(3)   **The Mystical or Illuminated View:**
       "...sees the writers of the Bible as Spirit-filed and guided believers, just as any believer may be even today."

---

[5] Charles C. Ryrie, *A Survey of Bible Doctrine* (Moody Press, Chicago, IL, 1972) pp. 38-40.

(4)   **Dictation View:**

…"verbal inspiration is that it means dictation; that is, the writers were completely passive and God simply dictated to them what was to be recorded. Of course it is true that some parts of the Bible were dictated (like the Ten commandments and the rest of the law), but [his] definition proposed above incorporates the idea that God allowed the writers varying degrees of self-expression as they wrote."

(5)   **Partial Inspiration Views:**

"…certain parts of the bible as supernaturally inspired, namely, portions which would otherwise have been unknowable…"

(6)   **Concept Inspiration:**

"…only the concepts but not the very words were inspired."

(7)   **Neoorthodox View:**

"…Barthian view…is that the bible is a witness to the Word of God…[and] is full of errors because it is merely the product of fallible writers."

(8)   **Inspired Purpose View:**

"…that while the Bible contains factual errors and insoluble discrepancies in its content, it does have "doctrinal integrity" and thus accomplishes perfectly God's purpose for it."

This author submits that every one of these views places a limit upon an Almighty Eternal God who exists as three persons, who is omniscient, omnipotent, and omnipresent, and who operates inside or outside the laws of nature and physics as we know them. Once again, *"inspiration"* is a miraculous process that is inexplicable in human terms. Any definition must yield to God's way of presenting it. It is a miracle. We should recognize and accept it by faith no less than we recognize the virgin birth, the resurrection, the ascension and many other Biblical miracles.

At the suggestion of Dr. Phil Stringer, various common dictionaries[6] were consulted to see if any commonly used definitions would match the use of *"inspiration"* in Scripture. This author could not find one dictionary that defined the word "inspiration" according to its Biblical use. What follows is the exegesis and definition of inspiration:

> *"**Inspiration** is* (1) **the miracle** whereby **the Words** of Scripture in Hebrew, Aramaic, and Greek were (2) **God-breathed** and **"once delivered"** using *"holy men of God"* and their vocabulary, (3) who perfectly **recorded** them **"once"** as they were *"**moved**"* along by the Holy Spirit (4) in such a way that *"**all**"* the Words written are **infallible and inerrant** in the sixty-six books of the canon of Scripture."

---

[6] The following dictionaries and MANY more were consulted: (1) *American Dictionary of the English Language, Noah Webster 1828;* (American Christian Education, San Francisco, CA, 8th edition, 1995); (2) *Webster's Student Dictionary, A Merriam-Webster* (G. & C. Merriam Co., Philippine Islands, 1938); (3) *Webster's Dictionary of the English Language*, Deluxe Edition (PMC Publishing Company, Inc. NY, NY, J. g. Publishing Co., Chicago, IL, 1992); (4) Encarta, English (North America) (Online Web Dictionary); (5) *The New Unger's Bible Dictionary*, (Moody Press, Chicago, IL, 1957); (6) *The Webster Reference Dictionary of the English Language, Encyclopedic Edition* (Publishers United Guild, Delair Publishing Co., 1983, (7) *Vine's Complete Expository Dictionary of Old and New Testament Words* (Thomas Nelson Publishers, Nashville, TN, 1976).

There were not "dual authors" of the Bible. There was one Author, *"the King eternal, immortal, invisible, the only wise God, be honour and glory for ever and ever."* (1 Tim. 1:17). A succinct way of stating the same thing is: **"The perfect author of the perfect Bible is God."**

If stated this way, one must understand the preceding four points. God did not "breathe-out" (1) any more or any less Words to be recorded as a product of *"inspiration"* than the canon of Scripture or (2) any translation of the Words into any receptor-language. The Words were *"once delivered"* by *"inspiration"* (Jude 3). The King James Bible states it better in a few verses than this author could ever express or sum up the Greek text that underlies it:

> *"All Scripture is given by inspiration of God..." (2 Tim. 3:16a) "Knowing this first, that no prophecy of the scripture is of any private interpretation. For the prophecy came not in old time by the will of man: but holy men of God spake as they were moved by the Holy Ghost." 2 Peter 1:20-21 "Beloved, when I gave all diligence to write unto you of the common salvation, it was needful for me to write unto you, and exhort you that ye should earnestly contend for **the faith which was ONCE delivered unto the saints."** Jude 1:3* (HDW, my emphasis, note that the word order in Scripture is for emphasis).

The result of inspiration is "revelation" of the "mind" of God in precise, infallible, and inerrant Words that man can understand, which are to act as absolute authority in all that pertains to life. The Words were provided because of God's grace. Accepting God's grace through faith leads to salvation: *"For by grace are ye saved through faith; and that not of yourselves: it is the gift of God:"* (Eph. 2:8), which results in the indwelling Holy Spirit in this dispensation. The Holy Spirit illuminates the Words for believers. Illumination is another miraculous process that helps sinful man to interpret the Words in context and apply them to life. The result of illumination is complete and utter awe of our Great God and Saviour, the Lord Jesus Christ, who is:

> "worthy... to receive glory and honor and power: for thou hast created all things, and for thy pleasure they are and were created." Rev. 4:11

What follows is an explanation of the Biblical use of *"inspiration"* **in context** and an examination of the fulfillment of God's promise to Preserve the inspired Words for *"the saints."* His promise of Preservation is so vast and extensive in Scripture that it cannot be denied except by the unbelief of unregenerate man.

There has not been an attempt to cover every aspect because it would take many books. There has been an attempt to repeat and emphasize certain precepts often. There will be no consideration given to the "pagan view," the "partial view," "natural view," or any view of *"inspiration"* of Scripture that does not recognize our Great God by His view of Himself presented in the Bible.[7] The Bible is God's love letter to man to explain man's failures and His hope for all men. This work is presented as a polemic for our brothers and sisters to turn to Scripture for understanding *"inspiration,"* and not rely on what other men say. It is recognized that the word, *"inspiration,"* is technically difficult to apprehend, but we must try.

---

[7] David Cloud, "Inspiration" (Way of Life Encyclopedia, Port Huron, MI, 4th edition, 2002) p. 292. Dr. Cloud discusses the three views in this section.

And when they heard that, they lifted up their voice to God with one accord, and said, Lord, thou art God, which hast made heaven, and earth, and the sea, and all that in them is: Who by the mouth of thy servant David hast said, <u>Why did the heathen rage, and the people imagine vain things?</u> Acts 4:24-25 (HDW, the underlined Words are from Psalm 2. David wrote the Words but the Holy Spirit (God) gave them)

"Wherefore (as the Holy Ghost saith), <u>To day if ye will hear his voice, Harden not your hearts, as in the provocation, in the day of temptation in the wilderness:"</u> Hebrews 3:7-8 (HDW, the underlined Words are from Psa. 95. David wrote the Words but the Holy Spirit gave them)

"Whereof the Holy Ghost also is a witness to us: for after that he had said before, <u>This is the covenant that I will make with them after those days, saith the Lord, I will put my laws into their hearts, and in their minds will I write them;"</u> Hebrews 10:15-16 (HDW, the underlined Words are from Jeremiah 31:33-34. Jeremiah wrote the Words but the Holy Spirit gave them)

CHAPTER 3

USE OF THE WORD "INSPIRATION" IN SCRIPTURE

The King James Bible uses the word, *"inspiration,"* in two places, Job 32:8 and 2 Timothy 3:16. The passage in Job in the Hebrew language indicates that man should be able to "know" and "teach" *"wisdom,"*[8] but only the Spirit can teach God's *"wisdom"* or *"revelation"* so that it may be understood spiritually. The reception and understanding of *"revelation"* can only be achieved through the agency of the Holy Spirit. Without the Spirit, spiritual 'things' can not be received or understood by men, even if they are *"aged"* or *"great men"* or *"wise"* (Job 32:9). The passage indicates that the Words of Scripture given by *"inspiration,"* which is *"wisdom,"* are received by certain men to be recorded for us. The men selected to record them are without consideration of being *"aged"* or *"great"* (Acts 10:34). Subsequently, their full understanding must come from God, the Holy Spirit.

The Apostle Paul recorded similar Words in Greek informing us that he was instructed and taught to *"speak...words"* that are *"spiritual things"* by the Holy Ghost. In other words, he received Words (wisdom) from the Holy Spirit which he spoke, taught, and preached and either he or his amanuensis recorded them *"once"* as they were God-breathed. He said:

---

[8] For the Biblical meaning of "wisdom," one must consider Biblical typology as seen, e.g., in Prov. 8 and 1 Cor. 1:17-31, particularly, verses 17, 21, 24, 30; the Lord Jesus Christ, who is the Word of God, is the "wisdom of God." These passages strongly suggest that the Words of God are wisdom.

*"Which things also we speak, not in **the words** which man's wisdom teacheth, but which the Holy Ghost teacheth; comparing spiritual things with spiritual. But the natural man receiveth not the things of the Spirit of God: for they are foolishness unto him: neither can he know them, because they are spiritually discerned." 1 Corinthians 2:13-14*

"Theopneustos" and the Greek Construction in Context

*"All scripture **(pasa graphe)** is given by inspiration of God **(theopneustos)**, and is profitable for doctrine, for reproof, for correction, for instruction in righteousness:"* (2 Timothy 3:16) (HDW, my addition).

Second Timothy 3:16 is **a very technical verse**. It was placed in Scripture to refute those who would claim: **(1)** only "parts" of the canon of Scripture are inspired, **(2)** inspired men wrote the words as coauthors, **(3)** an inspired message was given without regard to precise, perfect, infallible, inerrant Words, or **(4)** a translation of the God-breathed Words is inspired. In the context of all of Scripture, the God-breathed Words were given *"once"* by God to man as revelation.

A careful analysis (an exegesis in regard to all of Scripture) of the passage where this verse occurs counters these four false claims. A part of the problem today associated with interpretation of this verse concerns some **technical** grammatical features that some may not fully understand. **First**, the phrase translated *"by inspiration of God"* comes from one Greek word, θεοπνευστος, theopneustos, which is used in an adjectival position in this verse without the article "the." If the verse is translated as an attributive adjective with the article (which is not there in the underlying Greek text), then the verb, "is" would be placed **after** God and would read, "All given by inspiration of God is scripture." This construction would concur with those who believe only parts of Scripture are inspired. However, the Greek construction is a predicate adjective construction without the article "the," which requires the verbs "is given" **before** θεοπνευστος, which is appropriately translated syntactically as a prepositional phrase *"by inspiration of God."*[9]

Furthermore, a translation that reads like the NASB, NIV, or NLT such as "All scripture is God-breathed" by this construction leaves the open-ended question of deciding: "What are the **God-breathed Words?**" For example, "Is a translation called Scripture or the Word of God, in a receptor-language such as English, God-breathed?" or (2) "What parts of Scripture in the canon are inspired?" In other words, a person could again claim only a part of Scripture is God-breathed or a translation of the **God-breathed Words** are inspired. Only the KJB in context, particularly along with 1 Timothy 3:15, and all of the remainder of Scripture, allows the proper understanding that: all the Scripture (all the **God-breathed Words**) of the Bible in Hebrew, Aramaic, and Greek Words in the sixty-six books of the canon of Scripture *"is given by inspiration"* and *"once delivered"*(Jude 1:3) as the prophets and by extension, the Apostles, were *"moved by the Holy Ghost"* (2 Pe. 1:21).

---

[9] This verse is very difficult to express appropriately in the English language, but the KJB translators did an exceptional job even though they added some words not specifically found in the Greek text, such as "is given by." In the process they changed an adjective, theopneustos, to a noun expression, inspiration. But the verse fully understood as translated from the underlying text makes it clear that it was "all of God."

Explanation of "Moved" in 2 Peter 1:21

The word, *"moved,"* is from the Greek Word, phero, which in this verse is synonymous with being driven or being led by the Holy Spirit. Pastor D. A. Waite, Th.D., Ph.D., gives this excellent explanation of "moved" in 2 Pe. 1:21:

> "The definition of *"moved"* as used in 2 Peter 1:21 is the following. Of the 18 times the word, *"moved,"* is used in the New Testament, the Greek Word underlying it in 2 Peter 1:21 is unique. The word translated *"moved"* in this verse is **PHERO**. It means many things, but the specific meaning in this verse is *"to carry or move along as a sail boat is moved or carried by the wind."* The meaning of **PHERO** is further illustrated in Acts 27. As in Acts 27:15 *"And when the ship was caught, and could not bear up into the wind, __we let her drive__."* **PHERO** is the word which is used here. The ship was unable to be controlled either by the rudder or by the sails. It was at the mercy of this powerful wind and was simply *"carried or borne along."* Again in Acts 27:17, *"Which when they had taken up, they used helps, undergirding the ship; and, fearing lest they should fall into the quicksands, strake sail, and so __were driven__."* The Word which is used is **PHERO**. In this case, they *"strake sail"* and *"were driven, carried, or borne along"* by this fierce wind, totally unable to do anything in order to control the ship. In Acts 27:27, *"But when the fourteenth night was come, as __we were driven up and down__ in Adria, about midnight the shipmen deemed that they drew near to some country;"* In the words, *"__we were driven up and down__"* the word used is **DIAPHERO** which is a compound of **PHERO**. The ship was *"driven, carried, or borne along"* by that strong wind. The meaning of *"__moved (PHERO) by the Holy Ghost__"* in 2 Peter 1:21, is graphically illustrated by the account of the tempestuous storm described in Acts 27 where that

little ship was under the complete control of that moving wind."[10]

Explanation of 2 Timothy 3:15

In 2 Timothy 3:15, Paul is referring to copies of the canon of the Old Testament in Hebrew and Aramaic that were Preserved to the "jot and tittle" (apographs) and were available to Timothy for salvation. Then, he explains in verse 3:16 why the canon of Scripture was preserved in copies and available for salvation. The reason is because "all" the Words of Scripture in the original languages are God-breathed (autographs) by a miraculous process. The Words were not God-breathed in English, Spanish, French, Italian, German, etc., but were God-breathed in Hebrew, Aramaic, and Greek.

Theologians call this "verbal, plenary inspiration," which refers to all the Words in Hebrew, Aramaic, and Greek *"given by inspiration of God"* and *"once delivered."* It is a miraculous process. Some men claim only parts of the Bible are *"given by inspiration of God."* The Scripture does not indicate anywhere or in any part that the Words are limited or restricted in any sense. As a matter of fact, the Apostles, prophets, and our Lord's own Words affirm the verbal, plenary *"inspiration"* of the canon of Scripture, which cannot be explained in this short work. There are many works available that link other passages in Scripture to the doctrine of "inspiration" and preservation.

One of our present day scholars, Dr. D. A. Waite, Th.D., Ph.D., confirms these doctrines in his many works and a scholar in the past, Dean John William Burgon, affirms them also. In Dean Burgon's book, *Inspiration and Interpretation*, written in 1861, he said:

---

[10] A personal communication to this author from Pastor D. A. Waite, Th.D., Ph.D. concerning the meaning of "moved" in 2 Pe. 1:21.

> "But this day's Sermon,...has had for its object to remind you, that THE BIBLE is none other than *the voice of Him that sitteth upon the Throne!* Every Book of it,—every Chapter of it,—every Verse of it,—every word of it,—every syllable of it,—(*where* are we to *stop?*)—every letter of it—is the direct utterance of the *Most* High*!* Pasa graphé theopneustos. "Well spake the Holy Ghost, by the mouth of" the many blessed Men who wrote it.—The Bible is none other than *the Word of God:* not some part of it, more, some part of it, less; but all alike, the utterance of Him who sitteth upon the Throne; --absolute,--faultless,--unerring,--supreme![11]

"Inspiration" of the Words is complete, full, and perfect. Furthermore, the doctrine of verbal, plenary *"inspiration"* has been the dogma in the church since the early post-Apostolic era (q.v.).[12] All the Words in the passage, 2 Timothy 3:15-16, influence this conclusion when compared to each other and to the context of the whole Bible. Again, the unparalleled equivalent translating over a total of 7 years[13] by the King James Bible translators is seen by their precise handling of these verses through the method of verbal, plenary, formal, equivalent translating. The task of translating is not easy and can not be done quickly. The method and art of translating must be carefully

---

[11] Dean John William Burgon, *Inspiration and Interpretation* (Dean Burgon Society Press, Collingwood, NJ, 1999, originally published 1861 by J. H. and Jas. Parker) p. 89.

[12] This author recognizes that these specific words (verbal, plenary, infallible, inerrant) were not always used by authors down through the centuries, but were gradually added to help explain what has been meant by the Preserved Word/Words of God and refute apostate and heretical views. See Ryrie, op. cit., pp. 40.

[13] This author realizes the three committees that met at Cambridge, Oxford, and Westminster occurred during the latter part of this time period, but obviously those selected to participate began preparing during the interim before coming together.

performed. It requires great meditation, prayer, MANY *"counsellers,"* knowledge of cultures and languages, patience, longsuffering, money, and time. It is hard work that must be done diligently, throughly, and conscientiously.

Pasa Means "All," Not "Every"

The Greek πᾶσα (pasa), translated *"all"* in 2 Timothy 3:16, is used with an anarthrous (without an article such as "the") Greek noun, γραφή (graphé), which is translated *"scripture."*[14] It is well documented that this construction is translated "all" and not "every" (see Mat. 3:15, Acts 2:36, 7:22, Col. 4:12).[15] *Young's Literal Translation, The Amplified Bible,* and *Darby's Translation* inappropriately translate pasa as "every." The translations using "every" leave the door open for man to select what is, or is not, considered Scripture.

The Greek Word, Graphe, Means the Writings

Graphe is a technical word which is used to refer to the writings of Scripture, **not the writers** (cf. Jn. 5:39, Acts 17:2 Rom. 1:2 with Mat. 21:42, Jn. 13:18, Gal. 4:30). You cannot have writings without Words. In **2 Timothy 3:15**, the Holy Spirit, speaking through Paul, uses the Greek word, γραμματα (grammata) in a phrase: *"he hagia grammata,"* which is translated *"the holy scriptures."* Grammata refers to the temple's **copies** or **apographs** of the Old

---

[14] H. E. Dana and Julius R. Mantey, *A Manual Grammar of the Greek New Testament* (The Macmillan Co., New York, NY, 1927, © 1955) 149ff.
[15] Dr. Thomas Strouse, Dean, Emmanuel Baptist Theological Seminary EBTS), "The Translation Model Predicted by Scripture" (*EBTS Online Resources,* http://www.emmanuel-newington.org/seminary/resources/) p. 2.

Testament Scriptures to the *"jot and tittle."* The Greek word, *graphé* in **2 Timothy 3:16** refers to the **autographs** or the **original Words in Hebrew and Aramaic.**[16] The passage is clear that the Old Testament Words *"given by inspiration of God"* in the autographs were still present in the Apostolic era as apographs. By extension, and by the acknowledgement in Scripture by the Apostles and prophets that their Words were Scripture, the New Testament Greek text is included also (q.v.).

Some authors conclude that Timothy used Greek translations of the Old Testament and more specifically the Septuagint. This can not be substantiated. First, Timothy's mother was a Jew. Jewish mothers exerted a great influence in the home. Jews characteristically learned the Jewish language and Greek during the Apostolic era. Also, Timothy traveled with Paul, who visited Jewish synagogues. Surely, the "Law" was read from the Torah in Hebrew. For anyone to claim that Timothy did not know Hebrew and read only "copies" of the Greek translation in order to attribute *"inspiration"* to translations in the meaning and exegesis of 2 Timothy 3:15-16, is pushing history and accuracy of facts. Furthermore, **if** the Septuagint (LXX) existed as a complete translation of the Old Testament, and it probably did not, it was a VERY poor paraphrase, which Paul would have known.[17]

Dean John William Burgon succinctly points out that in 2 Timothy 3:16 there is no Greek eta, (**H**) between pasa and graphe. The significance is that the word "that," if an eta were present, would be placed in the verse to read: *"All Scripture that is given..."* Burgon said:

---

[16] Strouse, op. cit., ("The Translation Model Predicted by Scripture").
[17] H. D. Williams, M.D., Ph.D., "The Character of God's Words Is Not Found In the "G"" (DBS Message Book, #15 in a Series, July 2005) p. 24.

"St. Paul does not say that *the whole* of Scripture, collectively, is inspired. More than *that:* what he says is, that *every writing,*—every *several book* of those ἱερὰ γράμματα, or Holy Scriptures, in which Timothy had been instructed from his childhood,—is inspired by God...St. Paul is careful to remind us that every Book in the Bible is an inspired Book.[18]

These very purposeful **technical** verses, 2 Timothy 3:15-16, were given to Paul to record. They are carefully constructed verses by the Holy Spirit to defend the verbal (Words), plenary (all the Words), inspiration of Scripture given in Hebrew, Aramaic, and Greek as *"**the** foundation"* (i.e. translations of those Words are not the foundation). **The understanding of the technical verses, 2 Timothy 3:15-16, in English, Spanish, German, etc. cannot be garnered without the understanding and comprehension of the original inspired Words in Hebrew, Aramaic, and Greek Preserved by our God. The original Words in Hebrew, Aramaic, and Greek that lie behind the King James Bible are Preserved so that we might have recourse to them as a** *"foundation."*

---

[18] Dean John William Burgon, *Inspiration and Interpretation* (Dean Burgon Society Press, Collingswood, NJ, originally published 1861, republished 1999) 53.

"Now we have received, not the spirit of the world, but the spirit which is of God; that we might know the things that are freely given to us of God. Which things also we speak, not in the words which man's wisdom teacheth, but which the Holy Ghost teacheth; comparing spiritual things with spiritual." 1 Corinthians 2:12-13

CHAPTER 4

THE PROCESS AND PRODUCT OF "INSPIRATION"

The **"process"** of *inspiration,* the receiving of the God-breathed Words by the Apostles and prophets, is poorly understood by many of the saints because none of us has ever received "inspired" Words of God to be recorded as Scripture (2 Tim. 3:16, 2 Pe. 1:19-21, 3:2, Eph. 2:20) through the miraculous process of *"inspiration."* The **"product"** of *inspiration* is obvious; it is the original **Words** in Hebrew, Aramaic, and Greek recorded by the Apostles and prophets. It is the end result of the miracle of *"inspiration"* and is a part of *"inspiration."* In addition, *inspiration* and Preservation are about the Words, because:

> *"Heaven and earth shall pass away, but **my words*** (given by inspiration) *shall not pass away." Matthew 24:35* (HDW, my addition).

The end result of "inspiration" will be a message, but a specific message, resulting from specific, miraculous, perfect Words received to be recorded in sixty-six books, *"once delivered."* The conclusion of the miraculous process ended with the recording of the Words *"given by inspiration of God."* "Inspiration" does not extend to providential preservation or to translating the Words, but certainly these two aspects are linked to:

Go ye therefore, and teach all nations, baptizing them in the name of the Father, and of the Son, and of the Holy Ghost: Teaching them to observe all things whatsoever I have commanded you: and, lo, I am with you alway, even unto the end of the world. Amen.
Matthew 28:19-20

The product of *"inspiration"* is not a translation into the receptor-languages of the world. This can easily be demonstrated by examination of various translations throughout the centuries. They are not perfect. For example, the Syriac Peshetta is a translation that is based upon the TR/TT. In 1 Timothy 3:16 in several Syriac versions it has "he was manifest in the flesh" instead of *"God was manifest in the flesh."* In one translation, it has the following:

"and truly great, is this mystery of righteousness, which was revealed in the flesh, and justified in the spirit, and seen by angels, and proclaimed among the Gentiles, and believed on in the world, and received up into glory." (The Syriac New Testament, Murdock Translation,[19] 1 Tim. 3:16)

This translation is from the 9th edition in 1915 of James Murdock, D. D. from 1893. Which edition is "inspired"? Of course, none of them are "inspired" and it is insulting to the people of other receptor-languages to claim that only the English King James Bible is doubly or derivatively *"given by inspiration of God"* (q.v.), although its accuracy and faithfulness is inferior to no other translation.

---

[19] James Murdock, D. D, *The New Testament or The Book of the Holy Gospel of our Lord and our God, Jesus the Messiah, a Literal Translation from the Syriac Peshitto Version* (Scriptural Tract Repository, Marshall Bros., Agents, London, John K. Hastings, Boston, MA 1893, 9th edition, 1915). 1 Timothy 3:16.

We Accept by Faith
the Miraculous Process of Inspiration

We must accept by faith the proclamations of Scripture concerning the reception and recording of **special** revelation *"given by inspiration of God"* to God's prophets and Apostles. The corollary doctrine of Preservation goes hand in hand with *"inspiration"* (Psa. 12:6-7, 1 Pe. 1:23-25, etc.). No amount of jockeying the context of many passages by some exegetes will *"cast behind"* anyone's back the outcome of *"inspiration"* (Neh. 9:26); that is, the Truth, which is the *"jot and tittle"* recording of the Words and subsequently their Preservation. Theories must be cast aside! God did not try to hide the message only to be understood by mystics, 'scholars,' or teachers. The plan of God that the literal plain interpretation of Scripture is intended cannot be denied.

> "therefore, the literal method must be accepted as the basic method for the right interpretation in any field of doctrine today."[20]

Other "literal" verses teach the process of "inspiration" as men were *"moved by the Holy Ghost"* to record the Words in the autographs, the Words on the original manuscripts, which is the product of *"inspiration."* The following verses confirm that the Scriptures are the "literal" Words of God received by the Apostles and prophets from the Holy Spirit, not their interpretation of the Words.

---

[20] J. Dwight Pentecost, *Things to Come, A Study in Biblical Eschatology* (Academie Books, Zondervan Publishing House, Grand Rapids, MI, 1958) 33 (cf. pp. 16-34).

"knowing this first, that no prophecy of the scripture is of any private interpretation." 2 Peter 1:20 ""For the prophecy came not in old time by the will of man: but holy men of God spake as they were moved by the Holy Ghost" (2 Peter 1:21).

Paul records his knowledge that the Words he recorded were inspired and that their source was the Holy Spirit. He said:

"Which things also we speak, not in the words which man's wisdom teacheth, but which the Holy Ghost teacheth; comparing spiritual things with spiritual" (1 Corinthians 2:13).

Peter identifies the Words given to Paul by the Holy Spirit to record as Scripture. He said:

"As also in all his epistles, speaking in them of these things; in which are some things hard to be understood, which they that are unlearned and unstable wrest, as they do also the other scriptures, unto their own destruction" (2 Peter 3:16).

We find the OT prophets were repeatedly commanded to record the inspired Words describing a vision, commands, dream, etc. (Ex. 17:14, 34:1, 27, Deut. 10:2, Jer. 30:2, Hab. 2:2). Many excellent books relate the overwhelming references in Scripture to the doctrines of inspiration and preservation.

The Model For Making Copies

The model for Preservation of the inspired Words is also included in the Bible. **God made the first copy of His inspired Words.** He copied the exact same Words that were on the first tablet containing the Ten Commandments (Ex. 34:1). He also commanded Jeremiah to make a copy of the **exact** Words He gave him to record in the scroll that King Jehoiakim destroyed by cutting with a penknife and then burning the manuscript (Jer. 36ff).

Many good theologians do not express *"inspiration"* completely, which includes the process of *inspiration* as well as the product of *inspiration*. This leaves the door open for people to declare God has preserved His message, but not every precise Word perfectly; that is, to the *"jot and tittle."*

"Sanctify them through thy truth: thy word is truth." John 17:17 "And ye shall know the truth, and the truth shall make you free." John 8:32 "If the Son therefore shall make you free, ye shall be free indeed." John 8:36

CHAPTER 5

THE INFLUENCE OF HIGHER AND LOWER CRITICISM

The erosion of belief in the orthodox doctrine of *"inspiration"* by **(1)** the apostate and heretical higher and lower modern critics along with **(2)** the almost universal acceptance of evolution has almost led to total abandonment of the doctrine of perfect *"inspiration"* and preservation. For example, the almost universal acceptance of the theory of evolution has led most institutions of higher learning, including established Biblical schools, to view the Genesis account of creation and miracles as myth or allegory. Charles F. Kraft said:

> "Clearly, then, the Book of Genesis is a remarkable combination of ancient folklore, tradition, custom, myth"...Is the astounding story of the marriage of the 'sons of God' and the 'daughters of men' not ancient folklore to explain the origin of giants, 'Nephilim," on the earth in prehistoric time...?"[21]

Modernists such as Kraft, Bruce Metzger, and many others cast theories such as the JEDP Theory,[22] which is also known as the Graf/Wellhausen Theory, before students and pompously claim that

---

[21] Charles F. Kraft, *Genesis: Beginnings a Biblical Drama* (Woman's Division of Christian Service Board of Missions, The Methodist, 1964) pp. 11-12. This is quoted by David Cloud in "Biblical Inspiration, Part 1," Way of Life Literature, FBIS, 1994 from Way of Life Encyclopedia.

[22] This theory claims that the book of Genesis was written by four different authors. The theory has been "exploded" by many competent authors and its validity soundly defeated.

they are true. Furthermore, as neo-evangelicalism,[23] which started with Fuller University in California, *Christianity Today*, and Billy Graham, spread through our universities and schools in the mid-twentieth century, the doctrine of *inspiration* was softened or rejected. Subsequently, the emerging church arose and men began to latch onto and promote the claims that (1) only certain parts of Scripture were important to emphasize, or (2) the Scriptures were only a part of the revelation, the other part being a literal hearing of God's voice. In other words, God's personal communication with a believer was as important as Scripture and could act as revelation. They seemed to forget:

> "And this voice which came from heaven we heard, when we were with him in the holy mount. We have also **a more sure word of prophecy; whereunto ye do well that ye take heed**, as unto a light that shineth in a dark place, until the day dawn, and the day star arise in your hearts:" 2 Peter 1:18-19 (HDW, my emphasis).

These tenets would eventually lead to the apostate postmodern emerging church's false approach to evangelism and the Biblical doctrines of church administration and organization.[24] Included in postmodern theology is a rejection of the omniscient, omnipotent, and omnipresent God of the Bible in favor of a god who is ever learning.

---

[23] Neo-evangelicalism's basic tenet is the rejection of the Biblical doctrine of separation from apostasy and heresy in the hope of winning some. This is contrary to Scripture.
[24] H. D. Williams, M.D., Ph.D., *Hearing the Voice of God* (The Old Paths Publications, Cleveland, GA, 2007) See chapter 6, "Postmodernism," pp. 213-271. Also see, David Cloud, *What is the Emerging Church?* (Way of Life Literature, Port Huron, MI, 2008).

Obviously, the Biblical doctrine of *"inspiration"* can not stand or be tolerated in such an environment.[25]

Furthermore, many men are couching their definition of *"inspiration"* by coloring or altering what they mean by *"inspiration,"* because:

> "We must warn that many today who use the term inspiration, and who speak of an inspired Bible, do not necessarily mean that the Bible is the absolutely perfect Word of God...Dr. David O. Beale, in writing of the doctrinal battles which are raging in the Southern Baptist Convention, speaks of the deceptiveness of those who use the term "infallible Bible" apart from a historical definition of such:
>
> > "The doctrinal guideline for the [Southern Baptist] Peace Committee is the Baptist Faith and Message, a statement of faith adopted by the SBC in 1925 and revised in 1963. Article one of the statement says that the Bible HAS truth, without any mixture of error.' Fundamentalists, to the contrary, have always maintained that the Bible IS 'truth, without any mixture of error.' One can readily see that the Baptist Faith and Message is actually a protector of liberals, who would of course agree that truth has no mixture of error. That is a far cry from asserting the Bible is totally and absolutely inerrant. Much more significant, however, is the fact that liberals are being acknowledged as conservatives, simply because they use the word 'inerrant' to describe the Bible. Actually, they are using what Francis A. Schaeffer called 'a new loophole.' They readily use the word inerrancy, but they do not define the word in its historic, orthodox sense. Says Schaeffer, 'There are those within

---

[25] David Cloud, "Biblical Inspiration" (Way of Life Encyclopedia, Port Huron, MI, 4th edition, 2002) pp. 292-306. By "absolutely perfect Bible," this author is assuming David Cloud is referring to the autographs or the TR/TT text behind the King James Bible.

evangelicalism who are quite happy to use the words "infallibility," "inerrancy," and "without error," but upon careful analysis they really mean something quite different from what these words have meant to the church historically' (Schaeffer, *The Great Evangelical Disaster*, p. 56). The use of these words will, no doubt, save the jobs of many SBC seminary professors. <u>A recent article in SBC Today describes at least six different current usages of the word inerrancy: critical inerrancy, limited iner-rancy, qualified inerrancy, nuanced iner-rancy, functional inerrancy, and absolute in-errancy. Only the last one is the orthodox view, but liberals often do not explain their own use of the word</u> (Beale, "The Southern Baptist Convention's Ongoing Battle," *The Baptist Bulletin*, Sept. 1986)." [26]

Overreaction to Extreme Beliefs

In reaction to these attacks and many more, an attempt to counter them has been made by good soldiers of the Lord. This author believes that some good men have gone too far in opposing these scurrilous attacks. They have erred by going beyond the Biblical definition in an attempt to defend the *"inspiration"* of Scripture. This author understands the displeasure directed toward obviously unregenerate men who have done much to usher this age toward the days of Armageddon. However, we must not overreact to the point that sanctified believers add to the Scripture what is not revealed.

We plead for calmness, peace, civility, and patience among brothers in Christ as we work through the differences and the discussions of the issues surrounding *"inspiration"* of the Words of God" over the next few years. There is much material on the subject of

---

[26] Ibid. p. 297-298. (Way of Life Encyclopedia).

"inspiration" in the literature that extends from the early post-Apostolic era to the present age. We could not in one lifetime review it all.

Our plea is that men who have held certain positions will not be insulted or believe that THEY are being attacked. However, there are positions that are untenable according to Scripture such as: (1) no part of Scripture is inspired, (2) parts of scripture are inspired, or (3) a translation is inspired. In case number three, perhaps it is a matter of definition, but if so, it causes confusion. We do not claim to have all the answers. We do claim that the answers are in Scripture, but as sinners, none of us always sees clearly on this side of glory. We do not claim that every word written in this document will be understood the same by the author and by those reading it. Anyone who has written anything for public review will attest to the difficulty of covering "all the bases." But, the author would very much appreciate feedback and comments.

Therefore, in an attempt to assuage disagreements and accusations, certain words must be defined as documented above so that the author and reader are hopefully 'on the same page.' Certainly, it is difficult to express all that needs to be said in a brief work. Thousands of pages would be necessary. It is this author's primary hope that how he uses certain words will help toward the mark of "unity" concerning the proper use of *"inspiration."* Our aim as believers is not to please others, but to honour and glorify our Lord and His matchless Words that determine *"the faith"* *"once delivered"* by *"inspiration"* *"unto the saints"* (Jude 3).

A Few Definitions

(1) In this work, **"inspiration"** means **"God-breathed"** from the Greek word theopneustos (2 Tim. 3:16). It was a miraculous process that resulted in a miraculous product that has not been duplicated since the Scriptures were completed with the recording of the Words of the book of Revelation. The Words originally given in Hebrew, Aramaic, and Greek to selected, special *"holy men of God"* to record were "God-breathed." They are perfect as defined in this work (q.v.).

(2) Idealism means 'belief in perfection' of men or the products of men.

(3) Perfection or **perfect**[27] IN THIS WORK means without sin, **incapable of error of any sort,** faultless, infallible, pure, without blemish, without spot, or without ANY contamination and therefore, complete. This author believes that such **strong terms** as these should only be applied theologically to God and His God-breathed Words. Otherwise, calling something "perfect" may cause someone to claim man or something produced by man is equal to: **(A)** Our "perfect," sinless God who only could act as the *"perfect," "without blemish,"* and **"without spot"** "Lamb of God;" or **(B)** His "inspired" infallible Words, which were given *"once"* to man by *"inspiration"* as a perfect *"foundation"* for ever.

---

[27] Perfect in the King James Bible may carry **any** one of these following meanings in the Hebrew and Greek text from many different words. The context is the determining factor. Therefore, it is necessary in a brief work to precisely define what is meant by "perfect." The principle words used in the Bible are: Strong's 8549, 8552: entire (literally, figuratively or morally); also (as noun) integrity, **truth:--without blemish**, complete, full, **perfect**, sincerely (-ity), sound, **without spot, undefiled**, upright(-ly), whole. Strong's 5048, 5046 to complete, i.e. (literally) accomplish, or (figuratively) consummate (in character):--consecrate, **finish**, fulfil, make) **perfect**. the point aimed at **as a limit**, i.e. (by implication) the conclusion of an act or state (termination (literally, figuratively or indefinitely), result (immediate, ultimate or prophetic), purpose); specially, an impost or levy (as paid):--+ continual, custom, end(-ing), finally, **uttermost**.

(a) In the King James Bible, perfect may mean complete or undefiled in the sense of *"without spot," "without blemish,"* incapable of error, or sinless, as in Deut. 32:4, Psa. 18:30, James 1:17.

(b) In many other places, the context demands a sense of sinful man being complete, mature, or whole as in 2 Timothy 3:17, but retaining the capacity for sinning or of being influenced by sin. Paul clearly relates that he had not reached perfection, and if the great Apostle Paul had not, others have not either (Phil. 3:12).

(c) In the writings of some authors, perfect often means complete or mature or based upon the proper textual source, but that is not the way perfect is defined in this work.

(4) **Plenary** means **"all"** or complete and full and not limited in any respect.

(5) **Infallible** means **incapable** **of error.**

(6) **Inerrant** simply means **without error** or mistake. We hesitate to use this strong word for the King James Bible because of various revisions over the years; although this author believes the translating of the King James Bible by the guidance of the Holy Spirit was without any translational errors. But it had mistakes in printing, orthography, etc. (see below), which seems to be the plague of this author and others.

(7) **Verbal** means **the words**. Therefore, verbal, plenary simply means "all the words."

(8) **Formal** means a noun is translated for a noun, a verb for a verb, a pronoun for a pronoun, etc. so far as syntax of a language-group will allow.

(9) Equivalence = corresponds, sameness (meaning of a word) (e.g. a dozen is equivalent to twelve). This is synonymous translating. For example, there may be 7 or 8 synonymous receptor-language words, but only one was chosen to translate an original-language Hebrew, Aramaic, or Greek Word. Equal implies exactly the same. Translations are not equal to the *"once delivered"* Words *"given by inspiration of God."*

(10) Equal = the same, identical (word)(e.g. twelve = twelve).

(11) Error = mistake, blunder, inaccuracy, inexactness, confusion by disagreement of parts of Scripture; the antonym is accuracy.

(12) Translations vary depending on the method chosen to translate (e.g. verbal, formal equivalent (FE) **versus** dynamic equivalent (DE) or interpretive translating). The words chosen by man to translate the original 'received' inspired Words in the original languages of Hebrew, Aramaic, and Greek may be accurate, faithful, and without translational errors if they are translated by FE, but the words may not be perfect as defined in this work secondary to four reasons:

(1) Printing mistakes;

(2) Orthographic mistakes;

(3) Words chosen to translate an original-language word accurately and faithfully can be considered without error, but not so perfect that another word might **not** possibly be used (see equivalence above). This is synonymous translating, which may or may not be accurate, because all synonyms do not carry the same signification. The King James Bible translators were superior skilled linguists, but they expressed the possibility that another word with the same "sense" (e.g. a synonym) might be possible to use in translating an "inspired" Word and even

included some of them in the margin of the KJB.[28] In an accurate, faithful translation in any language, a synonym substitution or change could be found to be better in future revisions. This is the reason for some revisions. This author does not know of ANY translation that has not undergone either a revision or another edition.[29]

(4) The rules of grammar when translating to properly express the meaning may vary from the original-language texts (Hebrew, Aramaic, or Greek) to the receptor-language (English, Spanish, etc.). For example, a particle may be translated as an imperative as in Mat. 28:20. This is in contrast to the original Words 'received' *"once"* because they were perfect in every sense, grammar included. God gave them perfectly the first time they were recorded as revelation by the Apostles and prophets to act as a *"foundation."* An accurate and faithful translation that is without translational errors may be called the Word of God in English, Spanish, French, Latin, etc., but it is not the inspired Word of God, which was given *"once"* and should not be referred to as inspired or given by inspiration because of the confusion it generates.

Lastly, before a translation is released to the public, those responsible for a translation should be as certain as possible that it is correct. It should not be subjected to constant or frequent manipulation by revisions or editions. This causes confusion comparable to the multiple modern version fiasco. The properly

---

[28] Preface to the King James Bible, section, "Reasons Moving Us to Set Diversity in the Margin, Where There is a Great Probability of Each."

[29] Dr. Phil Stringer, *Ready Answers, A Response to the Evangelical and Fundamentalist Critics of the King James Bible* (Faith Baptist Church Publications, Ft. Pierce, FL) pp. 7-16. Also, see the information provided by Pastor Reagin in *The Lie That Changed the Modern World, A Refutation of the Modernist Cry, Poly-Scripturae* (Bible For Today Press, Collingswood, NJ, 2004) 338ff

translated KJB words should never be changed for these reasons in addition to the fact that it is an unparalleled English work in history.

Please refer back to these definitions as this sinner saved by grace tries to offer a clear explanation of a topic that is separating many good and godly men, which should not be the case. Brothers and sisters in Christ should be unified (Eph. 4:11-16). Many acknowledge the extreme difficulty of expressing spiritual things with words and therefore **must receive** the incredible gift of God's Words in Hebrew, Aramaic, and Greek as being superior to any word chosen by man.

The Words chosen by man to translate God's Words into another langauge may be watched over by God the Holy Spirit, but the idea that those words, which are chosen by man, are perfect (as defined in this work) or equal to the inspired Words is untenable. The Scripture given in the original Words was God-breathed by a miraculous process. The Holy Spirit's superintendence of a translation is no different than His assistance to sanctified pastors, missionaries, evangelists, teachers or saints preaching the Words of God. Hopefully, no individual attributes perfection, as it is defined in this work, to his preaching. However, the preaching of God's Words may be accurate, faithful, complete, mature, and without interpretive or translational mistakes or problems of application. If so, that kind of preaching can be called "preaching the Words of God." Anyone who has taught or preached knows that occasionally a wrong word or reference or similar is spoken, but it does not negate the other parts. This is similar to a printing or spelling error in a translation. The mistakes, like a printing mistake, do not negate the rest of the work or the preaching. The preaching or work can still be said to be accurate, faithful, and without **translational or interpretive** mistakes. However, it is not perfection as defined in this work. To hold a man preaching or a translation to such a high standard would be to insist that he is inspired, perfect, or breathing out words like God is capable of doing. Who has not made a slip of the tongue or wrongly quoted a verse? Man is not inspired and the words he speaks or writes are not inspired or perfect. Do any of you who are pastors, teachers, missionaries, or evangelists make the claim of perfection or *"inspiration"* of yourself or of the words you speak? Yet, you have often chosen words that translate or interpret the Words of God. Since you were called of God to your ministry, your preaching and teaching is superintended by God and you may be preaching or teaching the Words of God in English, or Spanish, or French, etc., but they are not inspired (God-breathed). Without a doubt, the blessings of God on the plenary, accurate, faithful, without **translational** errors King James Bible can be called the Words of God in English. I do not see how this could be denied. These concepts will be explained and repeated several times throughout this work and this author prays for understanding by the readers.

"God's Inspired Message to Man.

Scientific evidences to prove it!!!

"You may be surprised to learn that the Bible revealed that the earth is round. Job 26:10, Prov 8:27, Isaiah 40:22, Amos 9:6. Today, we chuckle at the people of the fifteenth century who feared sailing because they thought they would fall over the edge of the flat earth. Yet the Bible revealed the truth in 1000 B.C. 2500 years before man discovered it for himself!"

"Matthew Maury (1806-1873) is considered the father of oceanography. His wife was reading a portion of the Bible to him. While listening, he noticed the expression "paths of the sea" in Psalms 8:8. Upon his recovery, Maury took God at his word and went looking for these paths. We are indebted to his discovery of the warm and cold continental currents. His book on oceanography is still considered a basic text on the subject and is still used in universities. Maury used the Bible as a guide to scientific discovery. If only more would use the Bible as a guide in their personal lives!"

"The water cycle was not fully understood until about 30 B.C. by a Roman engineer named Marcus Vitruvius. Yet every aspect of the water cycle was fully revealed to mankind in 1600 B.C.! The Bible's description is in perfect harmony with modern science. Eccl 1:6-7; 11:3; Job 26:8; Amos 9:6. Vitruvius was 1600 years too late!"

(From: http://www.bible.ca/b-science-evidences.htm)

CHAPTER 6

A GLIMPSE AT HISTORY

The doctrine of verbal plenary *"inspiration"* has been one of the most widely held doctrines down through the centuries. Some men have tried to make the doctrine of verbal plenary inspiration a recent development. This claim can not be substantiated. Writing in the nineteen-fifties, Dr. R. Laird Harris said that there are those who claim that the doctrine of verbal plenary inspiration is:

> "a recent growth, the product of the Hodge-Warfield-Machen School of Princeton Seminary."[30]

The doctrine of *"inspiration"* is *not* "a recent growth" or claim about the Bible (q.v.). However, there is a battle raging today about the meaning of *"inspiration;"* a Biblical term. We are not talking about the common secular meaning of inspiration or inspired such as motivation, enthused, insight, moved, and similar things.

Where did this modern battle concerning Biblical *"inspiration"* begin? The most serious attacks originated in the mid-eighteen hundreds. Men began to widely publish the heretical theories of higher and lower criticism from 'scholars' and universities such as the school located in Tubingen, Germany. They were encouraged by the humanistic work, *On the Origin of Species* by Charles Darwin released in 1859. Anglican churchmen, Westcott and Hort, were particularly influenced by the work, which they believed could "not be answered."

---

[30] R. Laird Harris, Ph.D., *Inspiration and the Canonicity of the Bible* (Zondervan Publishing House, Grand Rapids, MI, 1957) p. 72.

After lower and higher textual critics like Westcott and Hort influenced the Committee of the Southern Convocation of the Anglican Church and numerous 'scholars' all over the world and particularly in America, Pandora's box of evil was opened. The attacks on *"inspiration"* intensified. The attempts to hold the assault in check would fail. The wounds from the attack were particularly evident in the Presbyterian denomination.

A Pivotal Point in the Battle For Biblical Inspiration

In the early nineteen hundreds, **one group** in the Presbyterian Church defended the *Westminster Confession of Faith* (WCF) recorded in 1646. They asserted that the doctrine of verbal inspiration had been held by the saints in sanctified churches since Apostolic times. They wanted churches to affirm (1) the inerrancy of Scripture, (2) the virgin birth and deity of Jesus Christ, (3) the doctrine of substitutionary atonement, (4) the bodily resurrection of Jesus, and (5) the authenticity of miracles. **A second group**, which produced the Auburn Affirmation in 1924, challenged the "Westminster" group's right to impose the five "fundamentals." The Auburn group argued that the Bible is not "an infallible guide" and that the "Westminster Standards" did not teach inerrancy of the Scriptures. The battle seems to have begun in the two influential seminaries of Auburn and Princeton. Phillip Schaff and C. A. Briggs of Princeton were apparently the instigators. Schaff wrote:

"the theory of a literal inspiration and inerrancy was not held by the Reformers."[31]

Of course, this is not true, nor is it true of the early church. The early church elder writings, as we shall demonstrate, as well as the WCF, speak about: (1) "infallible truth," (2) "nothing at any time is to be added" to the Scriptures, (3) the authority of Scripture "depends upon God (who is truth itself), the author thereof; and therefore is to be received, because it is the Word of God." In other words, the Scriptures are God-breathed (Greek, theopneustos), the Biblical definition of inspiration. The WCF speaks of the:

> "consent of all the parts," "The Old Testament in Hebrew...and the New Testament in Greek...being immediately inspired by God, and, by His singular care and providence, kept pure in all ages, are therefore authentical...the Church is finally to appeal unto them."

Three to four hundred years ago the claims of modern textual critics were in their infancy and were nowhere near the intensity of the attacks today. The alleged serious questions and conflicts of science and historical accuracy over the Bible had not yet arisen. Before these attacks began in the modern era, the authors spoke about:

> "the infallible truth" of the Word of God and this should be sufficient. "Inerrant" means "without mistake"; infallible means "incapable of error." It is actually a stronger word"[32]

---

[31] B. B. Warfield, "The Doctrine of Inspiration of the Westminster Divines" (This is from Warfield's work *The Westminster Assembly and Its Work* printed in 1931 which contains a reprint of his article.)
[32] Harris, op. cit., p. 73.

Similarly, the author of this work who defends the King James Bible (KJB), believes that **the KJB is without translational errors.** It does not contain **any errors or contradictions** as a result of translating. It does contain those mistakes of printing and spelling in the various editions so common in any product produced by man. The King James Bible does not contain any errors or mistakes or conflicts in its parts because it is an accurate and faithful translation of the infallible, inerrant Preserved Hebrew, Aramaic, and Greek Words *"given by inspiration of God"* by the method of formal, plenary, verbal, word-for-word translating. However, men are capable of error. Therefore, care must be exercised in calling any translation of the Bible infallible (incapable of error), or inerrant (without any errors), which are strong words by definition. Similarly, we must be careful calling a translation *"given by inspiration of God"* or "inspired" because of its Biblical definition. At the same time, we must understand:

> "that **the original writers of Scripture** were "indued with the infallible Spirit" and "might not err."[33] (HDW, my emphasis, indued means endowed, indue is now spelled endue).

In contrast, the apocryphal books are viewed by the WCF as mere "human writings," which are filled with errors (q.v.); therefore, they are not inerrant or infallible. Martin Luther did not accept the Apocrypha as canonical. Many authors before and after him also agreed. Similarly, many authors before and after Luther agree on the doctrine of *"inspiration"* espoused by the Lord Jesus Christ. As a matter of fact:

---

[33] Ibid. p.74. (Harris).

"The earliest writers know **no other doctrine**."[34]

Clement of Rome (c. died 101 A.D.) quoted from the Old Testament and attributes the Words "to God, Christ, or the Holy Ghost."[35] Clement said:

> "Look carefully into the Scriptures, which are the **true utterances of the Holy Spirit**. Observe that nothing of an unjust or counterfeit character is written in them."[36] (HDW, my emphasis)

From Clement on, the writers such as Ignatius (martyred c. 117 AD), Polycarp (c. 69-155), Tertullian (160-220 AD), Hippolytus (170-236 AD), and MANY others have affirmed these same beliefs about *"inspiration"* of Scripture. In essence, the Words are God-breathed; they are "without error in any part;" "they are infallible;" "the recorders have not erred;" and similar expressions. By the mid-nineteen hundreds, most universities and even seminaries had fallen under the spell of higher and lower critical theories. For example, Reinhold Niebuhr, a professor at Union Theological Seminary in New York, Wilhelm Pauck, a teacher at the Chicago Theological Seminary, E. C. Homrighausen of Princeton University, Edwin Lewis of Drew Theological Seminary, John Sutherland Bonnell, a Presbyterian minister of note, and G. Bromley Oxnam, a Methodist, began producing works denying inspiration or asserting claims such as:

> "the view that the Bible is infallible has largely died out among informed Protestants" and "except for a minority, Presbyterians do not believe in the literal inerrancy of the Scriptures" and "the virgin birth is not

---

[34] Ibid. p. 77. (Harris).
[35] Ibid. p. 77. (Harris).
[36] Ibid. p. 78. (Harris).

> used as a test of orthodoxy in receiving new members
> or in ordaining ministers and elders" and "With few
> exceptions...do not interpret the phrase in the
> Apostles' Creed 'the resurrection of the body' as
> meaning the physical body."[37]

The doctrine of verbal *"inspiration"* was then on the chopping block. Attacks from every angle were initiated. For example, *"inspiration"* was attacked from the position that it precluded the use of non-inspired documents such as genealogical records. *"Inspiration"* does not preclude that "homework" could not have been done by the Apostles and prophets prior to receiving the Words *"given by inspiration of God."* It is silly to believe otherwise. In other words, the Holy Spirit may have placed the desire in the Apostles and prophets to study documents, to speak with elders in the nation Israel, to seek out witnesses as the physician Luke did, and other comparable "homework" assignments before receiving by *"inspiration"* the precise, pure, perfect, infallible, inerrant, God-breathed Words.

The Depravity of Man

The Bible makes it clear that man is not perfect and cannot be perfect in this present world. Man is depraved (Jer. 17:9). This aspect of man is often called the *"old man."* After salvation and regeneration of the spiritual part of man by the indwelling of the Holy Spirit, the *"old man"* is still present and **battles** with the *"spiritual man."* The Apostle Paul acknowledged this battle (Rom. 7). Not only that, the Bible makes it clear that it is possible for man to change God's *"judgments,"* which were given by *"inspiration,"* into "gall" (i. e. depravity, Jer. 8:14, Am. 6:12, Acts 8:23). The great preachers of this

---

[37] Ibid. pp. 40-41. (Harris).

age such a Spurgeon, Edwards, Whitefield and others drove these facts home. They were preaching the Words of God accurately and faithfully. In these days, there is far too much "gall" (depravity) in preaching and in modern versions because they have not translated, interpreted, and applied the Preserved Words of God *"given by inspiration of God"* in Hebrew, Aramaic, and Greek by the method given in Scripture, word-for-word translating using the syntax of a receptor-language.

It seems that many of us do not get this message and believe that man is perfect after salvation. He is not. A man may be complete and faithful by being in Christ, but he is not perfect as defined in this work. He can do good things if he *"walks in the Spirit"* and follows the revealed will of God given by *"inspiration"* and properly translated and interpreted. This is an important message, because if man is not perfect (in contrast to the spotless Lamb of God), then he cannot cause or bring about something perfect. In order to do good as defined in Scripture, a man must *"walk in the Spirit"* by allowing the indwelling Spirit to direct him by the Words of God. Therefore, if a translator follows the method of translating given by God, which the KJB translators did, he will be empowered by the Holy Spirit to produce a translation that can be called the Words of God and without **translational** errors. Thus, the King James Bible is complete, accurate and faithful to the Words of God and can be said to be the Words of God in English without error, but this author does not believe it can be called inspired or God-breathed by derivative inspiration or given by double inspiration. Inspiration was a miraculous process that delivered the Words *"once."*

Humanistic Idealism

In the modern age, there is a large segment of academia that is touting "humanistic idealism" (perfection) which is 'one hundred and eighty degrees in the opposite direction' from Biblical idealism or perfection. Many are falling into the trap. The Bible declares man is not perfect as defined in this work. Secular or humanistic idealism is the sine qua non (Latin, absolute essential) of the atheistic *Humanist Manifesto:*

> "Humanism is a progressive philosophy of life that, without supernaturalism, **affirms our ability** and responsibility to lead ethical lives of personal fulfillment that aspire to the greater good of humanity."[38] (HDW, my emphasis).

But like most documents of man, the original *Humanist Manifesto* has undergone three revisions.[39] Therefore, man's "idealism" fails immediately. The humanist responds to this obvious contradiction by stating that man is "evolving" and once he is freed from the shackles of religion, man will progress toward an "idealist" state. The thinking of the humanist can be seen in the recent Christmas sign placed next to a nativity scene at the state of Washington's capital. The sign states:

> "At this season of the winter solstice may reason prevail. There are no gods, no angels, no heaven or hell. There is only our natural world. Religion is but a myth and superstition that hardens our hearts and enslaves our mind."

---

[38] http://www.americanhumanist.org/3/HumandItsAspirations.php
[39] Ibid. Humanist Manifesto III "For historical purposes, see preceding Humanist Manifestos: I and II."

Without a doubt, this statement is filled with hate and animosity toward God (Psa. 53). It is the hope of the atheist to remove any authority of a supreme being. This is the idealism (belief in perfection) of humanists.

The Believer's Idealism: Inspiration

In contrast, the idealism of believers is based upon the assurance of our *"hope"* by the revelation of God the Father in *"the great God and our Saviour, Jesus Christ,"* and by His revealed will received by *"inspiration"* (Jn. 14:10, 2 Tim. 3:16, Tit. 2:13); not by words breathed-out by man. The perfect, pure, inspired, infallible, inerrant (without error), eternal Words of God, were given *"once"* (Jude 3). They were given *"once"* in **perfection** by *"inspiration"* (2 Tim. 3:16). They will never need revision as any work of man would need. Translations of God's Words undergo frequent revision of the words and cannot be declared *"given by inspiration,"* which by definition means infallible (**incapable of error)** and inerrant (**without any error**.) If words are *"given by inspiration of God,"* they would **not** require editing or revision because of the specific Biblical definition of a **technical Biblical term**, *"inspiration."* The Holy Spirit, who is incapable of error because He is God, gave the Words. Dr. Harry E. Carr states it this way:

> "By inspiration, we mean the Holy Spirit selected each human author of the Scriptures and superintended them so that the writing was according to their personality and style, thus enabling them to record, **without error**, the Word of God. The word inspiration means God breathed.

> *"All scripture is given by inspiration of God,*
> *and is profitable for doctrine, for reproof, for*
> *correction, for instruction in righteousness:"*
> *2 Timothy 3:16*

"This indicates the method of transmission overseen
by the Holy Spirit.

> *"For the prophecy came not in old time by*
> *the will of man: but holy men of God spake*
> *as they were moved by the Holy Ghost." 2*
> *Peter 1:21*

"The Scriptures are "God breathed", which means that
their source is God. Holy men of God wrote them as
the Holy Spirit directed them. Each and every word of
the Scripture is inspired."[40] (HDW, my emphasis)

This is the true "ideal" that man needs to follow. The God-
breathed Words of God are true perfection; they are without spot or
blemish, incapable of containing any error, and are without error. But,
NO translation of the Scriptures has ever been perfect, **incapable of
error,** or **without error** of any sort from the very first edition or in
any subsequent revision. There are a few translations which meet
certain criteria, such as the proper text and the proper method of
translating the perfect Words of God, that can be declared to be
accurate, faithful, and without translational error, which is accurate
and faithful synonymous translating by word-for-word FE translating,
but man cannot declare that they were *"given by "inspiration of God"*
or perfect as defined in this work. The Words of God given by
"inspiration" as the *"foundation"* of our faith were given *"once"* without
error or capable of error.

> *"Beloved, when I gave all diligence to write unto you of*
> *the common salvation, it was needful for me to write*
> *unto you, and exhort you that ye should earnestly*

---

[40] Harry E. Carr, Th.D., Ph.D. *This I Believe, A Study in Systematic Theology,
Revised Edition* (Shalom Baptist Church, Orion, MI, 2004) p. 7.

*contend for **the faith** which was <u>**once**</u> **delivered** unto the saints." Jude 1:3 (HDW, my emphasis)*

Men Who Deny the Words "Once Delivered" and Preserved

In order to defend various positions (q.v. below), some individuals will immediately reply that we do not have any originals and we do not have any "perfect" copy of any of the original books of the Bible and therefore the Words in the copies cannot be declared inspired. For example, Dr. William W. Combs, Academic Dean of Detroit Baptist Theological Seminary wrongly reports:

> "It is the *original text* (words, script, autograph—*graphe*, 2 Tim 3:16) that partakes of inspiration proper. All other texts, copies, reproductions, translations, and versions partake of inspiration in an indirect, linear fashion from previous copies and translations to the extent that they reproduce the text of the original manuscripts. We hold that only the autographs of Scripture are inerrant and that copies and translations of Scripture are inerrant insofar as they are true to the inerrant autographs. Thus any translation or version of Scripture in any language is the Word of God if it accurately reproduces what is in the original manuscripts.
> "Thus, our Seminary statement limits inspiration primarily to the original manuscripts."[41]

Surely, he realizes the doctrine of *"inspiration"* cannot be separated from the doctrine of Preservation. The problem with this statement, which is similar to the proclamations of many authors, is

---

[41] William F. Combs, "Errors in the King James Version" (*Detroit Baptist Seminary Journal,* 4 (Fall 1999): 151–64)
http://www.dbts.edu/journals/1999/Combs.pdf, accessed 12/17/2008.

the failure to identify: (1) which text is the specific, inspired Preserved (capital "P") Words of God, and (2) which specific translation(s) is or are the preserved (small "p") Words of God. His fear must be the ridicule by other 'scholars' for maintaining that God fulfilled His promises of Preservation. If God did not fulfill his promise of Preservation, then the authority of God in all matters pertaining to life is moot. Many 'scholars' and Bible teachers proclaim that there are thousands of errors in the Received Text/Traditional Preserved Text. Have they not understood the words of 'scholars' far better trained, such as Dean John William Burgon, Edward Hills, D. A. Waite, Herman Hoskeir, and others? For example, Dr. Hills said:[42]

> "The texts of the several editions of the Textus Receptus were God-guided. They were set up under the leading of God's special providence. Hence the differences between them were kept down to a minimum. But these disagreements were not eliminated altogether, for this would require not merely providential guidance but a miracle. In short, God chose to preserve the New Testament text providentially rather than miraculously, and this is why even the several editions of the Textus Receptus vary from each other slightly. But what do we do in these few places in which the several editions of the Textus Receptus disagree with one another? Which text do we follow? The answer to this question is easy. We are guided by the common faith. Hence we favor that form of the Textus Receptus upon which more than any other God, working providentially, has placed the stamp of His approval, namely, the King James Version, or, more precisely, **the Greek text underlying the King James Version**."[43]

---

[42] David Cloud, "Correspondence With a Fundamentalist Baptist Teacher Who Denounces the King James Only Received Text Only Position" (Way of Life Literature, FBIS, 2001) see particularly pages 16-17.

[43] Edward F. Hills, *The King James Version Defended* (The Christian Research Press, Des Moines, IO, 4th edition, 1993) pp. 222-223.

The Words underlying the King James Bible is where we find the immutable, inspired, infallible, inerrant, Preserved Words of God. If Dr. Combs cannot identify these two texts, he cannot tell his students where the Words of God are to be found in the original and where the most accurate and faithful translation of them in English is located that can be called the Words of God in English (or any language). This is a significant failure of a teacher because the student will not have complete confidence in his Bible, nor will the student be convinced of a firm unchanging *"foundation"* that is his **absolute** authority (Psa. 11:3). In essence, Dr. Combs is essentially leaving the Words of God in "cyberspace" or in "all" the manuscripts. He has failed to confirm our Lord's promise to His students that:

> *"Heaven and earth shall pass away, but my words shall not pass away." (Matthew 24:35) "The words of the LORD are pure words: as silver tried in a furnace of earth, purified seven times. Thou shalt keep them, O LORD, thou shalt preserve them from this generation for ever." (Psalms 12:6-7) "Being born again, not of corruptible seed, but of incorruptible, by the word of God, which liveth and abideth for ever. For all flesh is as grass, and all the glory of man as the flower of grass. The grass withereth, and the flower thereof falleth away: But the word of the Lord endureth for ever. And this is the word which by the gospel is preached unto you." 1 Peter 1:23-25*

These promises are established in so many places by so many Words in Scripture that they cannot be twisted as so many 'scholars' try to do (q.v.). Without a doubt, God said it so many times and in so many ways in Scripture that any honest sincere student of God's Words appropriating this Truth would fall to his knees in adoration and thankfulness for His precious Words. Remember, His promises were signed and sealed by His amazing act of grace on the Cross of Calvary where His blood was shed. The blood was typically the ink by which His "testament" was signed, sealing it for ever (Heb. 9:16-26). This author cannot believe that God would subsequently let any of His "inspired" Words be unavailable to generations of saints by allowing the MSS to be hidden for hundreds of years in graves, the Vatican, or monasteries.

The only thing left for any saint to do is to identify where the text and translations are that were and are overseen by the providence of God the Holy Spirit. A sincere prayer to God for assistance will help any child of God to recognize them. The evidence is overwhelming, which is exactly what any honest man of God would expect. So, any text or translation built upon little evidence and constructed by apostate and heretical men should be suspect immediately. It would be honouring to the doctrine of separation to *"avoid"* texts produced by men who deny many clear, plain doctrines of Scripture.

Dr. Combs proclaims that only the original text (and no text existing today) can be called the Words *"given by inspiration of God"* and no manuscript can claim to be perfect or inspired because he claims no copy has ever been without error of any kind. No one knows this for certain; but we do know that the Words of God **accurately** copied **without error** do carry the original *"inspiration"* as it is defined in this work. **If the Words are copied exactly, they are the same Words that were God-breathed.** It would be ridiculous to claim the same Words when copied exactly, are not inspired. *"Inspiration"* is not dependent upon the material upon which the Words in Hebrew, Aramaic, and Greek are written, nor is *"inspiration"* dependent upon the recorders or the scribes who copied them.

Excellent, faithful men of God, superior students of God's Words, advanced linguists, and brilliant historians have one and all pointed to those matchless Words and where they can be found. Where are you looking? Are you looking at the corrupted texts of unregenerate men that were deniers of the divinity of the Lord Jesus Christ and the perfect infallible Preserved (large "P") Words of God given by *"inspiration"* and preserved (small "p") by formal, verbal, plenary equivalent translations? My plea to those of you on the wrong side of God's proclamations is to wake-up. Time is short. Cast aside pride and believe and trust God. Men in the past have admitted the error of their ways, such as Dr. Frank Logsdon. Check it out. Don't fall for the lies about him and others on the web or in a few articles. In the same Spirit of Christ, why don't you join with him and many of us who have repented of having any doubt about the perfect Preservation of the Words of a Holy God? God's Words are not nebulous about all of these things:

> *"And if any man hear my words, and believe not, I judge him not: for I came not to judge the world, but to save the world. He that rejecteth me, and receiveth not my words, hath one that judgeth him: the word that I have spoken, the same shall judge him in the last day." John 12:47-48*

How could He rightly judge us if the *"foundation"* is not perfectly saved for man to study, know, and live by? Our God would be unjust. He would not be the just and the justifier (Rom. 3:26).

"The words of the LORD are pure words: as silver tried in a furnace of earth, purified seven times. Thou shalt keep them, O LORD, thou shalt preserve them from this generation for ever." Psalms 12:6-7 "For ever, O LORD, thy word is settled in heaven." Psalms 119:89 "Heaven and earth shall pass away, but my words shall not pass away." Matthew 24:35 "Being born again, not of corruptible seed, but of incorruptible, by the word of God, which liveth and abideth for ever. For all flesh is as grass, and all the glory of man as the flower of grass. The grass withereth, and the flower thereof falleth away: But the word of the Lord endureth for ever. And this is the word which by the gospel is preached unto you." 1 Peter 1:23-25

CHAPTER 7

THE EVIDENCE OF PRESERVATION

Here is another consideration about those specific Words which will judge us. How do we know that we have the exact Words originally given by *"inspiration"*? **First**, God promised that He would preserve them as recorded in **many** passages in the Scripture (Psa. 12:6-7, 119:89, Mat. 24:35, 1 Pe 1:23-25, etc.). God's promise should be enough, but **secondly**, He has also provided other significant evidence by His superintendence of His Words. It is the testimony of history. It is the testimony of the Old Testament and New Testament Words "kept" by those who were given the responsibility. Those "saints" assigned the job are the nation Israel and the sanctified churches (Rom. 3:1-2, 1 Tim. 3:15). The Lord Jesus Christ said:

> *If ye love me, keep[44] my commandments. John 14:15 (cf. 14:23, 15:10, Mat. 19:17, 1 Jn. 3:22, keep and do, Jn. 3:24).*

Do you love Him? Are you keeping His Words *"once delivered"* and *"given by inspiration of God"* in Hebrew, Aramaic, and Greek? The evidence of history is **<u>overwhelming</u>** by many infallible proofs that the "saints" have done it in the past and are doing it today.

We have MANY very early manuscripts (MSS), versions, lectionaries, and church elder writings that are filled with quotes going

---

[44] See Strong's 8104, Heb. shamar, 5341, natsar, Greek, 5083, tereo.

back to the Apostles and prophets that are copies of the same original Words *"once delivered"* by *"inspiration."* The MSS and quotes are vast and varied. They are from the nation Israel, many churches, cities, areas, and nations. Obviously, a few manuscripts have been purposefully tampered with and are not reliable (about one percent (1%), such as MSS Vaticanus, Sinaiticus, D, C, and Alexandrinus[45]), but the Words in ninety-nine percent (99%) of the MSS are easily recognizable. Furthermore, the differences within the ninety-nine percent (99%) of the MSS are easily resolved except for a few (less than nine are significant) according to several of the great "reviewers" of the "received" Words of God. Dean John William Burgon and his most capable assistant, Edward Miller, in addition to other significant and well trained scholars such as Herman Hoskeir and Edward F. Hills, are a few affirming their Preservation. There are **few** differences, other than spelling differences, in the various editions of the Received Text/Traditional Text behind the most accurate and faithful translations of the Words of God. Those Words were affirmed in 99% of MSS from the early post-Apostolic age.[46]

Tertullian (c.155–230 A.D.) refuted the claims very early in the apostolic age that all the MSS were corrupted by indicating that the **autoographs** (originals from the pens of the Apostles and prophets were still available) and he held copies. He said:

---

[45] H. D. Williams, M.D., Ph.D. *Origin of the Critical Text* (The Old Paths Publications, Cleveland, GA, 2008) pp. 138-139.
[46] For example, see Dean John William Burgon, *The Causes of Corruption of the Traditional Text of the Holy Gospels* (Dean Burgon Society Press, Collingswood, NJ, 1998, first published, 1896 by George Bell and Sons, London) p. 16. See Edward F. Hills, *The King James Version Defended* (Christian Research Press, Des Moines, Iowa, Reprint 1993, First Edition 1956) pp. 220-223.

"I hold sure title-deeds from the **original** owners themselves...I am the heir of the Apostles just as they carefully prepared their **will** and **testament**, and committed it to a **trust**...**even so I hold it**."[47]

And he said:

"run to the apostolic churches, in which the very thrones of the apostles are still pre-eminent in their places, IN WHICH THEIR OWN AUTHENTIC WRITINGS ARE READ, UTTERING THE VOICE AND REPRESENTING THE FACE OF EACH OF THEM SEVERALLY. Achaia is very near you, (in which) you find CORINTH. Since you are not far from Macedonia, you have PHILIPPI; (and there too) you have the THESSALONIANS. Since you are able to cross to Asia, you get EPHESUS. Since, moreover, you are close upon Italy, you have Rome, from which there comes even into our own hands the very authority (of the apostles themselves)" (Tertullian, *Prescription Against Heretics*).[48]

Clement of Rome said:

"Thus the humility and godly submission of so great and illustrious men have rendered not only us, but also **all the generations** before us, better; even as many as have **received** His oracles in fear and truth."[49] (my emphasis, HDW)

Dean Burgon said:

---

[47] H. D. Williams, M.D., Ph.D., *The Lie That Changed the Modern World, A Refutation of the Modernist's Cry: Poly-Scripturae* (Bible For Today Press, Collingswood, NJ, 2004) 116. This is a quote from Wilbur Pickering's book, *The Identity of the New Testament Church*, p. 108.

[48] David W. Cloud, *Faith vs. the Modern Bible Versions* (Way of Life Literature, Port Huron, MI, 2005) 74.

[49] Clement of Rome, "The Epistle to the Corinthians" (*The Master Christian Library*, Ages Software, Version 8, Rio, WI, 2000) Chapter 19, p. 26.

"...it will be perceived that a three-fold security has been provided for the integrity of the Deposit:— Copies,—Versions,—Fathers."[50]

And he said:

"**The Traditional Text,...has been traced back to the earliest ages** in the existence of those sacred writings...It is evident that the turning-point of the controversy between ourselves and the Neologian[51] school must lie in the centuries before St. Chrysostom. If, as Dr. Hort maintains, the Traditional Text not only gained supremacy at that era but did not exist in the early ages, then our contention is vain. That Text can be Traditional only if it goes back **without break or intermission to the original autographs**, because if through break or intermission it ceased or failed to exist, it loses the essential feature of genuine tradition...I claim to have **proved Dr. Hort to have been conspicuously wrong, and our maintenance of the Traditional Text in unbroken succession to be eminently right.**"[52] [HDW, my emphasis]

And he said:

"The one great Fact, which especially troubles him [HORT] and his joint Editor [WESTCOTT],—(as well it may)—is *The Traditional Greek Text* of the New Testament Scriptures. Call this Text Erasmian or

---

[50] Dean John William Burgon, *The Traditional Text of the Holy Gospels* (Dean Burgon Society Press, Collingswood, NJ, Originally published 1896, republished 1998 by the DBS) 23.

[51] Neologian is the term coined by Dean Burgon and Edward Miller for the Alexandrian or 'new' Greek text constructed by textual critics that culminated with Westcott and Hort.

[52] Dean John William Burgon, *The Causes of Corruption of the Traditional Text of the Holy Gospels Being the Sequel to the Traditional Text of the Holy Gospels, Vol. II* (Dean Burgon Society Press, Collingswood, NJ, 1896, reprinted 1998) 1-3.

Complutensian,—the Text of Stephens, or of Beza, or of the Elzevirs,—call it the 'Received,' or *Traditional Greek Text*, or whatever other name you please;—the fact remains, that a Text *has* come down to us which is attested by a general consensus of ancient Copies, ancient Fathers, ancient Versions."[53]

And in addition he said:

"Variety distinguishing witness massed together must needs constitute a most powerful argument for believing such Evidence to be true. Witnesses of different kinds; from different countries; speaking different tongues:--witnesses who can never have met, and between whom it is incredible that there should exist collusion of any kind:--such witnesses deserve to be listened to most respectfully. Indeed, when witnesses of so varied a sort agree in large numbers, they must needs be accounted worthy of even implicit confidence... Variety it is which imparts virtue to mere Number, prevents the witness-box from being filled with packed deponents, ensures genuine testimony. False witness is thus detected and condemned, because it agrees not with the rest. Variety is the consent of independent witnesses,... It is precisely this consideration which constrains us to pay supreme attention to the combined testimony of the Uncials and of the whole body of the Cursive Copies. They are (a) dotted over at least 1000 years: (b) they evidently [Burgon means by evidence, there is no doubt here, HDW] belong to so many divers countries,—Greece, Constantinople, Asia Minor, Palestine, Syria, Alexandria, and other part of Africa, not to say Sicily, Southern Italy, Gaul, England and Ireland: (c) they exhibit so many strange characteristics and peculiar sympathies: (d) they so clearly represent countless families of MSS., being in no single instance absolutely identical in their text, and certainly not being

---

[53] Dean John William Burgon, *The Revision Revised* (The Dean Burgon Society Press, Collingswood, NJ, originally published, 1883, reprinted 2000) 269.

copies of any other Codex in existence,--that their unanimous decision I hold to be an absolutely irrefragable evidence of the Truth."[54] [my addition, HDW]

In conclusion, we believe by faith that God Preserved His Words. It is a position that is not without overwhelming evidence. The printing press invention allowed men to more easily filter the **"virtually identical"** ninety-nine percent (99%) MSS group called the Textus Receptus or Traditional Text into one final text. This author believes the final edition was honed by approximately fifty great historically unmatched scholars and godly translators of the King James Bible. The Words in Hebrew, Aramaic, and Greek behind the King James Bible are the Words of God given *"once"* by *"inspiration."* History has affirmed God's blessings on this translation.

An Example

An example is necessary at this point. Many of you reading this document have been involved in constructing a building. The most important aspect of any building is the *"foundation."* When my wife and I built our home, we were approached by the contractor to consider various types of cement for the foundation. We were asked to decide whether to add fiber or rebar, a rod of iron. He reported that recently experts ('scholars') were recommending fiber to be added to the cement. Our simple question was which one had withstood the 'test of time'? His response was rebar. He said fiber was 'new.' We chose rebar. This account is similar to 'scholars' recommending 'new' English versions of the 'bible' based upon 'new' texts. Shouldn't we ask, "Which

---

[54] Dean John William Burgon, *The Traditional Text of the Holy Gospels, Vol 1* (The Dean Burgon Society Press, Collingswood, NJ, 1998) 50-51.

version has withstood the test of time?" Without a doubt, it is the King James Bible and the Hebrew, Aramaic, and Greek text that underlies it that has been blessed. The test of time reaffirms our belief that for the English-speaking world, the King James Bible is the most accurate, faithful, translation without **translational** errors of the Preserved Words of God given by *"inspiration."* **It is the *"rod of iron"* in the English language**.

"Because I will publish the name of the LORD: ascribe ye greatness unto our God." Deuteronomy 32:3 The Lord gave the word: great was the company of those that published it. Psalms 68:11 How beautiful upon the mountains are the feet of him that bringeth good tidings, that publisheth peace; that bringeth good tidings of good, that publisheth salvation; that saith unto Zion, Thy God reigneth! Isaiah 52:7

CHAPTER 8

THE VARIOUS POSITIONS OF MEN

In addition to the confusion of terms, there are also definite diverse positions regarding *"inspiration,"* some of which are strongly held. Furthermore, the positions and the men holding to various texts and translations are frequently misrepresented.[55] The debates over the last several centuries can be tied to: **(1)** several distinct original language texts in Hebrew, Aramaic, and Greek and **(2)** the translation of those texts, which are **all** claiming to be the Words of God.

Some of those positions can be tied to man's desire for *idealism* (the achievement of perfection) in this life, which is theologically impossible. We know that we will not be free from sin until we are 'glorified' with our Lord in Heaven (Phil. 3:21, 2 Cor. 1:10); therefore the works of man will not be perfect (as defined in this work!). Some may immediately claim that the Holy Spirit causes some works of man to be perfect by His superintendence or watchful

---

[55] The frequent misrepresentation of individuals can be seen in the following works: Dr. Michael D. Sproul, *God's Word Preserved* (Whetstone Precepts Press, Tempe, Arizona, 2005) pp. 35-39. Also see: James D. Price, *King James Onlyism, A New Sect* (Published by James D. Price, printed in Singapore by Saik Wh Press, PTE. LTD. ISBN 978-0-9791147-0-0, 2006) pp. 15-18. James R. White, *The King James Only Controversy, Can You Trust the Modern Translations?* (Bethany House Publishers, Minneapolis, MN, 1995). James B. Williams, Randolph Shaylor, Editors, *God's Word in our Hands* (Ambassador Emerald International, Greenville, SC, 2003. These works are particularly wrong about the various definitions of "King James Onlyism" and those individuals holding the positions.

guidance. No passage in Scripture affirms this untenable position of "perfection" in man (as defined in this work!). Man may do "good" works and **may** have the possibility of being "perfect" (incapable of error), but neither man nor his works are perfect because of sin (2 Tim. 3:17).[56] We are to strive for perfection, but we have not reached it; even the great Apostle Paul confessed his failure to reach perfection although it was his "ideal."

> *"Not as though I had already attained, either were already perfect: but I follow after, if that I may apprehend that for which also I am apprehended of Christ Jesus." Philippians 3:12 (cf. Phil. 1:6)*

Ideologically, **man** uses "idealism" in many ways. For example:

(1) In relation to the Scripture, idealism implies without sin or the state of sinlessness. It may have reference to the state of man prior to the fall. It would be an "ideal" state, but it is no longer achievable secondary to the "fall of man." Unfortunately, many individuals believe that after salvation they are no longer sinners. That would be ideal, but of course, it is a false position and contrary to Scripture. This work cannot explore the Biblical answer to this false position, but many theological works investigate why this is not true from a sound Biblical point of view.

(2) The term "Biblical Idealism" is sometimes used as: **(a)** a reference to an occurrence, an idea, concept, type, or representation in prophecy that repeatedly occurs in history. It is often an appeal to treating the Scripture as allegory. **(b)** It may refer to an

---

[56] Some may recognize the preceding discussion as the failure (sin) of man **until** the final stage of salvation, glorification, when we will be free from the presence of sin. Please note that 2 Tim. 3:17 states "***may be*** *perfect;* " it does not say **is** perfect.

event that actually occurred or existed, such as Babylon's destruction, which is touted as an event that is repeated throughout history. For example, Hitler's downfall in Berlin is an "ideal" occurrence and is a reoccurrence of Babylon's fall. **(c)** Others wrongly believe that Jesus' second coming occurred in 70 AD (preterism) and allegorically is continuing to happen every day in the lives of some men.

(3) In philosophy (the study of wisdom), idealism is understood to be an impossible goal to obtain when faced with the reality of the world, but that the "imperfect reality" (the world) **reflects** the invisible ideal. Philosophers, such as Plato (429-347 BC), have:

> "postulated the existence of a realm of Ideas that the varied objects of common experience imperfectly reflect. He maintained that these ideal Forms are not only more clearly intelligible but also more real than the transient and essentially illusory objects themselves."[57]

George Berkeley (1665-1753 AD), Immanuel Kant (1724-1804), George Wilhelm Frederick Hegel (1770-1831), and others continued a philosophical foray into the concepts of idealism. Ultimately, philosophers conclude some truth(s) **separate from** what believers in the Lord Jesus Christ consider the absolute Truth, the Bible. In other words, for philosophers, an ideal realization can be achieved by dialectical interaction, logic, or *"critical analysis"* of the material or real world. Philosophical beliefs of this nature, which ultimately stemmed from the unholy Greek triumvirate of Socrates, Plato and Aristotle, were the great downfall of Biblical *textual critics* through the

---

[57] Encarta Encyclopedia, see
http://encarta.msn.com/encyclopedia_761575556_1____2/Idealism.html#s2
or http://encarta.msn.com/encyclopedia_761551873/Dialectic.html

centuries. Men such as Origen, Bengel, Semler, Griesbach, Westcott, and Hort were involved in scholastics (mixing Greek philosophy with the Bible). Westcott and Hort made Greek philosophy the centerpiece of their reading. They believed that they could establish the original text of Scripture by *"critical analysis"* and knowledge, a form of Gnosticism. God clearly rejects such thinking by recording for us:

> *"For my thoughts are not your thoughts, neither are your ways my ways, saith the LORD. For as the heavens are higher than the earth, so are my ways higher than your ways, and my thoughts than your thoughts." Isaiah 55:8-9*

God calls man's words, *"lying words"* and *"chaff"* (Isa. 32:7, 59:13, Jer. 7:8, Jer. 23:28). Obviously, Old Testament leaders in Israel were taking God's Words and interpreting (translating) them to benefit their lusts. This tendency persists into modern times.

Translational Idealism

(4) **"Translational Idealism"** is related to the belief that certain translations of the Bible have reached or are equivalent to the **perfection** of the 'received' original Words of God and can be called "inspired." This is "idealism" that stems all the way back to Plato et al. The conclusion that a perfect translation as defined in this work or even a perfect 'original' text can be achieved by **reasoning** is the result of the *"logic"* or the *"critical analysis"* of men. This is the **reasoning of men** that was first heralded by Platonism, but it is inappropriate.[58]

---

[58] "Platonism provided Christianity with its unique Gospel of Redemption, with a universal theoretical foundation of mysticism: in the great process by which the world comes forth from God and returns to God, through the Logos or knowledge of God."

It is a result of "idealism" or "idealistic" goals. Many individuals may not realize that their claims of a "perfect" or "inspired" ideal translation(s) stem from Greek philosophy. According to Scripture, this cannot be. First, man is depraved; he is a sinner. Secondly, in a *"born-again"* man, the old man is still present (Eph. 4:22, Rom. 7:13-25). Words chosen by man to translate the 'received' Words of God may **reflect** the original perfect "ideal" Words that are God-breathed, but they are **not** the God-breathed Words. This concept is similar to the doctrine that a born-again man may be complete, but certainly not equivalent to the *"perfect"* indwelling Holy Spirit, the Lord Jesus Christ, or the Father. A man is never perfect or equal to any one of the three persons of the Trinity, just as translated words are never perfect or equal to the *"once delivered"* inspired Words.

Many will immediately jump to the conclusion that this author believes that the King James Bible has errors. It does not have any translational errors, although many opponents of the KJB have tried their best to prove a translational error. They have been unable to demonstrate any true errors except for printing, orthographic, singular words recorded as plural words (and vice versa), the omission of a phrase or word, and occasional translational differences (e.g. word inversions), which I do not consider translational errors. Dr. Edward F. Hills concurs with this position.[59] Errors of disagreement between parts, confusion of precepts, of fact, of contradictions, of serious anomalies or aberrations have never been demonstrated in the KJB.[60] The modern versions are rife with these problems and cannot be considered as **not** having translational errors. The King James Bible is

---

http://encarta.msn.com/quote_561552486/Philosophy_Platonism_provided_C hristianity_with_its_.html?partner=orp
[59] Hills, op. cit., p. 230.
[60] Williams, op. cit., pp. 335ff.

without translational errors in all its particulars because it is based on the proper text, proper method of translating, and proper art of translating.[61] The fact that it is a translation removes it from the category of an inspired text (q.v.); that is, God-breathed Words, given *"once,"* and from every possibility that it is inspired.

Some very important scholars who are far better than many so-called 'scholars' today and who have defended the King James Bible do not believe that the KJB is inspired. Dr. Edward F. Hills (1912-1981), speaking about the KJB, said:

> "Admittedly this venerable version is not absolutely perfect, but it is trustworthy."[62]

Which text is "perfect"? Irenaeus (c. 115-202 A.D.) knew. He was a student of Polycarp, who in turn was a student of the Apostle John. It is the Words "uttered by" the Holy Spirit. He said:

> "...The Scriptures are perfect, inasmuch as they were uttered by the Word of God and His Spirit."[63]

Furthermore, the translated Words may **reflect** the perfect Hebrew, Aramaic and Greek Words of God, but they are not the perfect Words. Translated Words may be accurate, faithful, and without error because they are based on the proper text, but they are not perfect as defined in this work. The whole of Scripture indicates that there are

---

[61] The "art of translating" is the experience that translators can bring to the method of word-for-word translating (VPT) that is dependent upon knowledge of cultures, at least the original languages and a receptor-language, sanctification, linguistics, Bible knowledge and many other factors. A computer is not adequate for this aspect.

[62] Hills, op. cit., p. 230.

[63] Hills, op. cit., p. 2. Hills quoting Irenaeus from Migne's *Patrologiae Cursus Completus, Series Graeca*, vol. 7, col. 805, col. 844.

only four perfect gifts from heaven: (1) The Lord Jesus Christ, who is God, (2) The Holy Spirit, who is God, (3) The Father, who is God, and (4) The Hebrew, Aramaic, and Greek Words of God, *"forever settled in heaven"* that came down from heaven (Psa. 119:89, James 1:17, 3:15, 17) *"once."*

> *"Every good gift and **every perfect gift** is from above, and cometh down from the Father of lights, with whom is **no** variableness, neither shadow of turning." James 1:17, cf. 3:15, 17 (HDW, my emphasis)*

There is *"no variableness, neither shadow of turning"* in the Trinity or the Words of the Trinity. The Words are perfect as defined by this work and have no spelling errors, no "printing" errors, and no interpretations. They were recorded as *"holy men of God...were moved along by the Holy Ghost"* (2 Pe. 1:20-21). A translation is **variable** and shows a *"shadow of turning"* through editions and revisions.

An Example

The tabernacle in the wilderness was an accurate and faithful *"shadow"* or **representative** of the true tabernacle in heaven. It was constructed from the pattern given to Moses on the Mount. It was a true **representation** of the heavenly tabernacle. Therefore, God accepted it as set aside, sanctified, or holy to Him (Ex. 29:43, 40:34). Otherwise, He would not have accepted it. A proper translation is an accurate, faithful **representative** of the true Words given by *"inspiration."* The tabernacle in the wilderness was set aside (holy) to God, but it was not free from the presence of sin (consider Lev. 10:1-2, 1 Sam.2:28-34). In addition, why else would it have been necessary for the Lord Jesus Christ to ascend into heaven to the 'true' tabernacle to sprinkle His perfect blood on the mercy seat?

A proper translation is set aside (holy) to God, but it is not infallible, incapable of error, by virtue of the fall of man, although it may be without translational errors. God gave the design of the tabernacle in heaven, just as he gave the design to the *"jot and tittle"* of the Words *"forever settled in heaven"* in Hebrew, Aramaic, and Greek. Man is **commanded** to make the Words known by translating them with Words that are accurate and faithful **representatives** of the original words that have been Preserved to the *"jot and tittle."* The Apostle Paul said:

> *"But now is made manifest, and by **the scriptures** of the prophets, according to the **commandment** of the everlasting God, **made known to all nations for the obedience of faith:**" Romans 16:26* (HDW, my emphasis).

In other words, *"the scriptures"* were translated. The Lord said:

> *"In the law it is written, With men of **other tongues and other lips** (languages) will I speak unto this people; and yet for all that will they not hear me, saith the Lord." 1 Corinthians 14:21 (HDW, my addition).*

He speaks to men through accurate and faithful translations of Scripture. The method of translating is also clearly given in Scripture, which is word-for-word (e.g. Mat. 1:23, Mr. 5:41, 15:34, Jn. 1:38, 41, etc. interpreted = translated).

CHAPTER 9

"INSPIRATION"
IS A HIGHLY TECHNICAL TERM

The original Hebrew, Aramaic, and Greek Words of God <u>from heaven</u> were supernaturally given to man by *inspiration,* **a highly technical Biblical term** (Psa. 119:89, Dan. 10:21, 2 Tim. 3:16). Although this topic has been touched upon previously, the **results** of the technical aspects have not been clearly delineated. Many have failed to recognize and fully apprehend the Biblical term and the consequences of misunderstanding the concept.

No translation produced by logic, critical analysis, textual criticism or equivalence, whether formal, verbal, plenary or dynamic equivalency, could equal the matchless Words of God received **"once"** for *"obedience to the faith."* The perfect Words must be *"received"* (Jn. 17:8). This is similar to receiving the Lord Jesus Christ unto salvation. Both are related to faith—*"So then faith cometh by hearing and hearing by the word of God"* (Rom. 10:17) You cannot receive salvation without 'receiving' the Words of God as Truth through faith. The Preserved Words of God received by the **process** of *"inspiration"* and verbally, plenarily, accurately, and faithfully translated into a receptor-language without translational error can be called the preserved Words of God in English, Spanish, French, Africanis, etc. However, a translation can never be called inspired, a technical term, because the words are **chosen** by man to accurately and faithfully **represent** the Words given by *"inspiration."*

Dr. Phil Stringer makes this sagacious point:

"If a translation were inspired, it could be done within a few days because God would be breathing-out the words. Every accurate and faithful translation takes from a few to many years."[64]

The words chosen by the translator will not be "inspired," but if they are accurate and faithful, they will be inerrant and carry **the full authority** (q.v. see the discussion about authority below) of the perfect, pure, inspired, inerrant, infallible, Preserved Words of God. God's reputation (character) will stand behind them.

Properly Translated Words Possess the Properties of the Words of God

Without a doubt, the preserved Words of God through proper translating of the Preserved Words of God in Hebrew, Aramaic, and Greek possess the properties of **authority** outlined so clearly in Hebrews 4:12, which says:

"For the word of God is **quick**, and **powerful**, and sharper than any twoedged sword, **piercing** even to the dividing asunder of soul and spirit, and of the joints and marrow, and is **a discerner** of the thoughts and intents of the heart." Hebrews 4:12

Properly translated Bibles are:

(1) quick (alive),

(2) powerful (2 Tim. 3:16-17),

(3) piercing (providing signs, wonders, miracles, and gifts, Heb. 2:4), and

---

[64] A personal communication to this author.

(4) a discerner (Ecc. 8:5, Eze. 44:23, Mal. 3:18, 1 Co. 12:10).

Therefore, the Preserved Words of God in Hebrew, Aramaic, and Greek accurately and faithfully translated will carry **the authority** of the original perfect Words. But, the translated words are not derivatively inspired or doubly inspired (q.v.) because the Word "inspiration" is a Biblically technical term meaning **God-breathed**. It is used only ONCE in the New Testament. In other words, translated Words are not God-breathed, but they may be the preserved Words of God in a receptor-language (such as Spanish, English, German, French, etc.) if they are accurately and faithfully translated by plenary, verbal, formal equivalent translating using the method of "word-for-word" translating so far as the syntax of a receptor-language will allow.

There is ample evidence that translations are not inspired. They may have many printing errors, may have words that could be represented by another word, may be based upon the wrong text, and may have orthographic problems (spelling errors). To deny these things would be equivalent to calling black white or white black. Only the original Words given in Hebrew, Aramaic, and Greek that were recorded by *"holy men of God...as they were moved by the Holy Ghost"* (2 Pe. 1:21) are the inerrant, infallible, inspired, pure, perfect, immutable, eternal, and Preserved Words given by God through the methods mentioned below.

The God-Breathed Words Are a Product of a Miraculous Process.

The original God-breathed Words in Hebrew, Aramaic, and Greek are the result of a miraculous process. It is another miracle among many recorded in the Scriptures such as the iron axe floating, the virgin birth, the resurrection of Jesus Christ and His ascension, people raised from the dead, healed, or caught-up to heaven, manna from heaven, the calming of storms, and many others. Those Words recorded by this miraculous process produced a product (the written Words) that the prophets and Apostles recognized as Scripture.

The miraculous process which produced the product of *"inspiration"* ceased with the completion of the recording of the book of Revelation. One of the reasons exegetes (expositors) claim that revelation, and therefore Words given by *"inspiration,"* ceased after the book of Revelation was written is the proper exegesis of 1 Cor. 13:10. One must note the gender agreements in this verse in the Greek with "perfect." The word, "perfect," is a neuter word in Greek. Both heaven and Jesus Christ are masculine words so that the neuter word, "perfect" is not referring to them. However, the Greek word, biblia, meaning book (or bible) is neuter, agreeing with "perfect." Therefore, when the "perfect" Bible was finished, *"then that which is in part shall be done away."*

Furthermore, the prophets and Apostles realized that they were receiving "God-breathed" Words in Hebrew, Aramaic, and Greek that could be called Scripture. In 2 Pe. 1:20-21, Peter calls the prophet's writings, Scripture; in 2 Pe. 3:16, the Apostle Peter calls the Apostle Paul's Words, Scripture; in 1 Tim. 5:18, the Apostle Paul calls Luke's Words, Scripture. It was a miraculous process that no man since the Apostle John (the recorder of last book in the Bible, Revelation) has experienced. Lastly, 1 Cor. 2:11-16 indicates that we have *"the mind of Christ."* How could we have the *"mind of Christ"* without His recorded Words? They are *"the voice of God"* recorded for us and are sufficient and authoritative for all things pertaining to life.

Our Lord stated that the original Words in Hebrew and Aramaic were perfectly Preserved to the *"jot and tittle"* when He walked the face of this planet in the flesh (Mat. 5:17-18). Undoubtedly, the Words Preserved to the *"jot and tittle"* were copies (apographs of the autographs). Paul indicated the same thing to Timothy in 2 Timothy 3:15; that is, copies of *"the holy scriptures"* were Preserved Words and available to Timothy for salvation. The Lord Jesus Christ, who is *"the word of God"* (Jn. 1:1-2), indicated that His *"words shall not pass away"* or disappear (Mat. 24:35, cf. Mk. 13:31, Lk. 21:33) by the strongest negative, *"ou me,"* in the Greek language.

> *"Heaven and earth shall pass away, but my words shall not (Greek, ou me) pass away." Matthew 24:35*

By extension, His Words include *"all"* the Words recorded by holy (set aside, special) men in the canon of the Old Testament and the New Testament, which are *"forever settled in heaven"* (Psa. 119:89, 2 Pe. 1:20-21). The Words are one of the perfect gifts that came down from heaven; another perfect, sinless gift is the Lord Jesus Christ. The Words in Hebrew, Aramaic, and Greek were not *interpreted* by man and then recorded:

> *"Knowing this first, that no prophecy of the scripture is of any private interpretation." 2 Peter 1:20. "Every good gift and every perfect gift is from above, and cometh down from the Father of lights, with whom is no variableness, neither shadow of turning." (James 1:17, cf. James 3:15, 17)*

The Foundation

The inspired Words are the same Words *"yesterday, today and forever"* just as *"Jesus Christ the same yesterday, and to day, and for ever"* (Heb. 13:8). The Words of God that define Christian doctrine were received *"once"* without error (Jude 3). As the Words are copied down through history, the original Words given by inspiration that are accurately copied retain their inspiration. They are the exact same Words given *"once."* A man copying the Words is not inspired or *"moved by the Holy Ghost"* to copy the Words without error or in other words, perfectly. However, God insured their Preservation by creating the desire in the saints of the nation Israel and sanctified churches to copy the original perfect Words accurately and faithfully. He superintended their Preservation. He did not God-breathe the Words a second time or each time they were copied. The OT Words were guarded, watched over, protected and Preserved by the scribes in the nation Israel by VERY specific rules for copying.[65] The sanctified churches were scattered in many nations and the saints in those churches, who were indwelt by the Holy Spirit, would never intentionally corrupt the Words of God when copying. Thus, many manuscripts, versions in other languages, church elder writings, and lectionaries confirm the almost seamless, error free, "virtually identical" stream of Preserved Words from many areas that are found in the manuscripts.[66] These mechanisms are the ways in which God's original Words were Preserved in order to act as a **foundation** for translating. We must build on that foundation.[67] In other words, we must translate from that foundation. Just as God promised us that He would watch over their Preservation (Psa. 12:6-7, Mat. 24:25), we believe that He superintends the accurate and faithful translation of

---

[65] Pastor D. A. Waite, Th.D., Ph.D., *Defending the King James Bible, A Fourfold Superiority* (Bible for Today Press, Collingswood, NJ, 2006, 10th printing, 3rd revision) pp. 24-26.
[66] Dean John William Burgon, *The Traditional Text of the Holy Gospels, Vol 1* (The Dean Burgon Society Press, Collingswood, NJ, 1998 pp. 50-51.
[67] Waite, op. cit. pp. 18-19.

the original God-breathed Words as well. However, no amount of "idealism" will cause a translation to be or become a result of "inspiration."

In a private email to this author, Dr. D. A. Waite, Th.D., Ph.D. said:

> **We must be nailed down to Biblical definitions in all of our theological parlance.** I think of the popular definition of "inspire," "inspiring," inspired," and "inspirational" which are used about poems, songs, books, and other things. And then I think of the **Biblical definition of "inspiration" which is limited and closeted in 2 Timothy 3:16: "all Scripture (PASA GRAPHE) is given by inspiration of God (THEOPNEUSTOS)." It means all the original Hebrew, Aramaic, and Greek Words that were written down in the 66 books of the Old and the New Testaments were GOD-BREATHED. or BREATHED OUT BY GOD. There can be none other Biblical definition of the term of inspiration than this.** The doctrine of inspiration must be just as Biblically tied down and limited as any other major doctrine such as the deity of Christ, the bodily resurrection of Christ, the substitutionary death of Christ, the power of the Blood of Christ, the incarnation of Christ, or any other Biblical doctrine. We cannot and we must not define or redefine inspiration in any other manner than what the Bible does. **If we do, we are humanizing (and idealizing) this important definition much like the modernists and the neo-orthodox theologians do with Biblical words and doctrines,** or like John MacArthur does with the Blood of the Lord Jesus Christ."[68] (HDW, my emphasis).

Men influenced by "idealism," "idealizing," or idolizing are being prejudiced by man's reasoning, which emanates from Greek

---

[68] Dr. D. A. Waite, Th.D., Ph.D., from a private email to this author on 12/08/2008.

philosophy (q.v.). Without a doubt, man is commanded to translate the Words of God in order to make them known to other nations or language-groups for the "obedience of faith" (Rom. 16:25-26, 1 Cor. 14:21, Col. 1:5-6, Mk. 13:10). But a translation must come from the original foundational Words given by inspiration. The original Words were given for **a (one)** *"foundation,"* which by commandment are never to be altered (Deut. 4:1-2, Pro. 30:5-6, Rev. 22:18-19).

We may ask: "Why did God do it this way?" He could easily breathe-out perfect, inspired Words in any language, but He chose Hebrew, Aramaic, and Greek. We believe that He uses man to translate His *"foundation"* in order for man to study and learn His Words. Similarly, God could breathe-out absolutely perfect copies of His Hebrew, Aramaic, and Greek Words for every generation. He did not, so man must study and research for a purpose. What is that purpose? Man would be more likely to be able to commit to faithful men His Words and doctrine in a group-language such as French, German, Spanish, English, Swahili, Pigeon, or any other language (2 Tim. 2:15). The translated Words of the Preserved Words carry **the authority of God, IF** they are translated accurately and faithfully by verbal, formal plenary equivalent translation technique clearly outlined in God's Words (see below).

God's Method of Translating

God's instructions for accurate and faithful translating are in His Words that are given by *"inspiration."* The method of the translation of the Words of God is by word-for-word translating (Jn. 1:42, Acts 9:36, Heb. 7:2, etc., interpretation = translation). Nowhere in Scripture does He indicate that the Words which man translates into the languages of the world from the original Words are "inspired." The inspired Words were given only *"once"* by *"inspiration"* as a **foundation** for doctrine, examples, commandments, precepts, judgments, etc. The Apostle Paul, as a *"wise masterbuilder"* and one sent by God, said:

> *"saints…are built upon* **the foundation** *of the apostles and prophets, Jesus Christ himself being the chief corner stone;"* Ephesians 2:19-20. *"According to the grace of God which is given unto me, as a wise masterbuilder, I have laid* **the foundation***, and another buildeth thereon. But let every man take heed how he buildeth thereupon."* 1 Corinthians 3:10 *"Nevertheless* **the foundation of God** *standeth sure, having this seal, The Lord knoweth them that are his. And, Let every one that nameth the name of Christ depart from iniquity."* 2 Timothy 2:19 (HDW, my emphasis)

God promised that His Words would be Preserved, perfect, *"incorruptible,"* and available for ever (Psa. 11:3, Mat. 4:4, 24:35, 1 Pe. 1:23-25, 2 Pe. 1:21, Jude 3). Anytime a question arises in any translation of the Words into any language anywhere in the world, the **original Words** *"given by inspiration"* in Hebrew, Aramaic, and Greek are to be consulted as *"the foundation"* for a final determination; not another translation, and certainly not man's words as final authority. Rather, man is to reference the original Words given *"once"* and Preserved. The Words given *"once"* are *"the foundation"*!

"Perfection" Defined

No translation has reached perfection like the Words of God recorded by God's special designees (q.v.). The various books in the Bible do reflect the linguistic vocabulary of the prophets and Apostles, but this does not negate the selection or perfection of the Words by the

Trinity. It would be nothing for God to use the vocabulary of an individual. As Dr. D. A. Waite has said: "It is all of God." Here is the proof. The Words of God *"given by inspiration of God"* using a special *"holy man of God's"* vocabulary and recorded by a man, on occasion, were (1) not understood by the man selected to record them (e.g. Dan. 12:8). Yet, (2) the Words were recorded **without error.** These two facts give great credence to the doctrine that the Words *"once delivered"* were inspired and they were *"settled in heaven"* among the Trinity before they were given to man to record (Psa 119:89).

In the King James Bible, the word perfect may be *interpreted* as 'complete' or 'mature' in certain passages. In this work, perfection does not mean 'complete.' Therefore, in this work, translations may be plenarily complete, accurate, faithful, and without translational errors, but not perfect. If you are reading this document and you mean by your use of "perfect" that the KJB is accurate, faithful, and without translational errors, then we are in agreement. By this, one can see the importance of defining words accurately. Translations may be accurate and faithful to the original Hebrew, Aramaic, and Greek God-breathed perfect, infallible, pure, inerrant, Preserved Words, which were *"delivered once"* (Jude 3) and which have been, are, and will be *"the faith,"* the final authority, the foundation, the doctrines, and the beliefs for *"the body of Christ."* All too frequently, the modern textual debate uses the reasoning of men, which has led to a false "idealism" (perfection) in translations. Attributing perfection or inspiration to the building (the translation) based upon the inspired *"foundation"* approaches a type of mysticism that we see in the emerging church. This is similar to claiming **any** church built upon the foundation of the Apostles and prophets is perfect. Without a doubt, the third person of the Trinity, God the Holy Spirit, superintends the selection of words by sanctified God-believing individuals who are desirous of an accurate and faithful translation of the proper text by the proper method. That is why some translations retain the *"living water"* or Spirit of God (Jn. 7:38). Who has not read a 'new' modern version and discovered the Spirit missing? Furthermore, the confusion generated by 'new' versions is deeply disappointing.

The only perfect things that came down from heaven and exist **materially** (e.g. in the flesh or having a material existence) are the God-man, the Lord Jesus Christ and His Words. Even Adam and Eve were created in innocence, not perfection, with the possibility of being perfect (without sin). But by choice, they yielded to that old Devil in the Garden. Man, who is depraved as a result of the fall (Jer. 17:9), can choose words that **reflect** the words of God by the process of translation, but because of man's imperfection, the Words can only be complete, accurate, faithful, and without translational mistakes, but not perfect. Perfection begets perfection. Imperfection may **reflect** the perfect, but not be perfect; that is without spelling, printing, or similar deficiencies. Possibly, men who claim "inspiration" for the preserved (small "p") Words of God in a translation by accurate and faithful translating are confusing terms. If someone looks into a quiet stream, the reflection of himself is accurate and faithful, but not a perfect image in three dimensions. The perfect, inspired Words of God in Hebrew, Aramaic, and Greek are infinitely perfect and came down from the infinite dimensions of God (heaven).

Various Positions

Many authors in one way or another have identified their positions as:

1. A Critical Text (CT) Position: endorses the CT that was **constructed** by the method of choosing words by eclecticism and subjectivism from a few (about 5) corrupted MSS (primarily MS B); endorses translating of the CT as the Words of God and approves the modern versions based upon it.

2. A Majority Text Position: asserts the Words of God are to be found in "all" the manuscripts (MSS); the text is constructed allegedly from "most" of the MSS and is closest to the original. From this text, translations are made. There are two competing Majority Texts, which are: (1) the Robinson and Pierpont text (1991), and (2) Hodges and Farstad text (1982).

3. A Received Text or Textus Receptus/Traditional Text (TR/TT) Position: varies depending upon whether an individual supports,

> (A) a particular TR/TT edition of Erasmus, Stephens, Beza, or Elziver. Some individuals select one or the other.
>
> (B) an eclectic approach to the TR/TT, which is illustrated by those who continue to pick and choose words from the various editions of the TR/TT or
>
> (C) the single text believed to be the result of a purification process. This position is based upon the success of a single TR/TT edition that lies behind the King James Bible, which has succeeded beyond man's imagination or ability. In other words, it has been blessed mightily by God. This text is the 1598 edition of Beza with few exceptions.

4. An Inspired Translation Text Position: which can also be divided into several camps, which are:

(A) God directly inspired a translation such as the KJB and it can be used to correct the original language texts. This is a Peter Ruckman position called Ruckmanism. He has made the following statements:

"The A.V. 1611 reading, here, is superior to any Greek text" (Peter Ruckman, *The Christian's Handbook of Manuscript Evidence*, Pensacola Bible Press, 1970, p. 118).
"Mistakes in the A.V. 1611 are advanced revelation!" (Ruckman, *Manuscript Evidence*, p. 126).
"A little English will clear up the obscurities in any Greek text" (Ruckman, Manuscript Evidence, p. 147).
"If all you have is the 'original Greek,' you lose light" (Ruckman, Manuscript Evidence, p. 336).
"If you are able to obtain a copy [of Ruckman's proposed new book] you will have, in your hands, a minimum of 200 advanced revelations that came from the inerrant English text, that were completely overlooked (or ignored) by every major Christian scholar since 90 A.D." (Bible Believers' Bulletin, Jan. 1994, pp. 2,4).
"We shall deal with the English Text of the Protestant Reformation, and our references to Greek or Hebrew will only be made to enforce the authority of that text or to demonstrate the superiority of that text to Greek and Hebrew." (Peter Ruckman, Problem Texts, Preface, Pensacola Bible Institute Press, 1980, p. vii).
"Observe how accurately and beautifully the infallible English text straightens out Erasmus, Griesbach, Beza, Nestle, Aland, Metzger, Trench, Vincent, Davis, Wuest, Zodhiates, Elzevir, and Stephanus with the poise and grace of a swan as it smoothly and effectively breaks your arm with one flap of its wings. Beautiful, isn't it? If the mood or tense isn't right in any Greek text, the King James Bible will straighten it out in a hurry" (Ruckman, Problem Texts, pp. 348, 349).
[Editor: Why does Ruckman put critical, modernistic textual editors Nestle, Aland, and Metzger on the same level with Beza, Elzevir, and Stephanus who

honored the Word of God and handed down to us the
Text Received from the Apostles?]
"The King James test is the last and final statement
that God has given to the world, and He has given it in
the universal language of the 20th century ... The truth
is that God slammed the door of revelation shut in 389
BC and slammed it shut again in 1611" (Peter
Ruckman, The Monarch of Books, Pensacola, 1973, p.
9).

(B) Derivative inspiration, which states that a translated Bible receives inspiration from the underlying original Words. It ignores the Biblical definition of inspiration, theopnuestos (theos = God; pnuestos = breathed). This position also ignores the Bible's declaration that the Words of God were *"once delivered"* by *"inspiration." (Jude 1: 3)* The word order in the Greek text, as in the KJB, is for emphasis on "ONCE." The belief in derivative inspiration confuses the issue (i.e. what was *"given by inspiration"?).*

(C) Double inspiration, which means that God gave the words of the KJB translation by "inspiration." This position is so far out of the ballpark that it will not be considered in this work because Scripture indicates the inspired words were given *"once."*

(D) Translations from the TR/TT into the languages of the world are inspired.

Which Version of the
King James Bible Is Inspired?

Perhaps many teachers of God's Words do not realize that the first editions of the KJB contained the apocrypha; non-canonical books written during the 400 silent years between the completion of the Old Testament and the New Testament. The books of the apocrypha:

(1) are not in Hebrew;

(2) do not contain statements by the writers that would lead anyone to conclude the apocrypha was inspired (e.g. "the Lord spoke through me" or "these are the words of God");

(3) have never been acknowledged as Scripture by the Jews;

(4) were not used or allowed by Christian churches in the first four centuries;

(5) contain fabulous statements;

(6) have many doctrines that conflict with orthodox doctrines;

(7) teach immoral doctrines such as lying, suicide, assassination, etc. [69]

What about the versions of the King James Bible that contain printing errors? Men claiming inspiration of a King James Bible must answer critics' questions such as those found on the web in an article "Which King James Bible?":

> "Few people seem conscious of the fact that a currently circulating King James Bible differs in significant details (though not in general content) from the one issued in 1611. They assume that the King James is a fixed phenomenon like "the faith which was once for all delivered unto the saints" (Jude 3; ASV). However, a current KJV differs from the 1611 edition in numerous details. According to modern standards, books produced in the seventeenth century were carelessly printed. The 1611 editions of the KJV had "Then cometh Judas" in Matthew 26:36, which should have been "Then cometh Jesus." The second edition by dittography repeated twenty words of Exodus

---

[69] Pastor D. A. Waite, Th.D., Ph.D., *Defending the King James Bible* (The Bible For Today Press, Collingswood, NJ, 2006) p. 71-73.

14:10. The two editions of the KJV issued in 1611
differ from each other in several other respects.
Printers errors in various later printings created
oddities like the "Wicked Bible" (which omitted "not"
from the seventh of the ten commandments), the
"Unrighteous Bible" (in which the unrighteous inherit
the Kingdom), the "Vinegar Bible" (with its "Parable of
the Vinegar") the Ears to Ear Bible, and many
others."[70]

In this article, many other questions are raised. Some of them are easily answered, but the question, "Which King James Bible edition or revision is inspired?" cannot be answered. No pounding of the pulpit, threats, proclamations, emotional declarations, or similar can make the legitimate questions go away. Some mystical text that no one has ever seen or held in their hands is not tenable. Contemplative mysticism about the Words of God is a product of modernism, neo-orthodoxy, and trust in man rather than in a Rock solid *"foundation."* Furthermore, mysticism is the modern ecumenical approach of the emerging church to the Words of God.[71] God's special, called-out *"holy men of God"* recorded His Words perfectly. God promised their Preservation. History affirms the Preservation of the Preserved Words in Hebrew, Aramaic, and Greek. History affirms the accurate and faithful translation of them, but not the perfection of a translation. Belief in a perfect translation *"given by inspiration of God"* is the result of a tendency towards "mysticism."

---

[70] "Which King James Bible?"
http://www.asapnet.net/remnant/page5isKJVonly.htm accessed 12/17/2008.
[71] David W. Cloud, *Contemplative Mysticism, A Powerful Ecumenical Bond* (Way of Life Literature, Port Huron, MI, 2008) Many passages in this book present the mysticism surrounding the Words of God and mystical revelations.

The Greatest Failures

There are two significant failures or denials associated with several of the false positions above.

(1) The greatest failure of most positions is the lack of a specific definition for "inspiration," **a highly technical Biblical term** meaning God-breathed (q.v.).

(2) The second significant failure is the denial of perfect Preservation of the Words of God in Hebrew, Aramaic, and Greek as promised in the Scripture. Evidence of the Preservation of the 'received' Words of God abounds (q.v.).

Biblical "inspiration" is a VERY technical term. This cannot be stated enough because of the modern confusion concerning this word. Secular definitions, theories, or ideas cannot be used to define the term.

The following quote demonstrates how many individuals **deny** the Preservation of the inspired Words of God as promised by our God and recorded in Scripture in dozens of verses such Psalm 12:6-7, Matthew 24:25, 1 Peter 1 21-23, etc., It is a poor answer to the following good question in a book titled, *One Bible Only*:

> "Hasn't God promised to preserve all of the words of Scripture?"

> "Most careful interpreters would say that no such specific promise can be found in the Bible itself. In fact, even John Burgon—something of a hero to the King James-Only advocates—insisted that the Bible contains no promise of textual preservation. The passages that are supposed to contain this promise do not stand up to careful scrutiny. Without exception,

they appear to be talking about something besides the
written preservation of all of the words of Scripture."[72]

In my opinion, the authors of this quote go to **extremes** to
deny the Preservation of the Words of God by twisting the exegesis and
interpretation of the clear literal statements of Scripture. Furthermore,
they have not understood Dean Burgon's words in the context of all his
writings. Anyone can take "quotes" out of context and make them say
what they want. This author has had that happen to him. Who has not
encountered the 'saint' who has used a quote of Scripture out of
context? We must be careful when quoting. If an interpretation seems
to be in conflict with orthodox doctrine, particular care must be
exercised.

Obviously, Beacham et al. consider **their** convoluted, twisted
exegesis as the way God intends the Scripture to be evaluated or
interpreted. Nothing could be further from the Truth. Abundant books
by numerous authors have documented the Preservation of the
Hebrew, Aramaic, and Greek Words by the literal plain interpretation
of appropriate passages. Furthermore, many books have documented
their accurate and faithful translation into several languages of the
world. Those translations that are properly translated can be called a
Bible because they preserve the Words of God in a receptor-language.
In addition, numerous books demonstrate proper literal hermeneutics
of the Words of God as opposed to twisting the language as too many
modern exegetes have recently done.

---

[72] Roy E. Beacham & Kevin T. Bauder, General Editors, *One Bible Only?
Examining Exclusive Claims for the King James Bible* (Kregel Publications,
Grand Rapids, MI, 2001) p. 177.

CHAPTER 10

DERIVATIVE INSPIRATION

At this point, we must consider a frequent claim which cannot be validated from Scripture. It is the claim of derivative inspiration of a translated Biblical text. In the discussions to follow, the terms and concepts related to **innate** and **inherent** compared to **inherited** and **acquired** are important. The reader of this section would do well to keep a good competent dictionary close at hand.

God is an eternal being. He does **not** inherit or acquire abilities. He is **not** the product of a birth; he is **not** a creation. Therefore, God's power, authority, and characteristics are **inherent** or **innate** without any relationship to being born, created, or genetically made. His **traits** are inherent and not secondary to inherited abilities. His **power** and **authority** are not acquired or inherited; they are inherent. His abilities and character traits are **not** developed, learned, or conditioned by the environment. Therefore, we speak of God's power, authority, and knowledge as stemming from His omnipotence, omniscience, and omnipresence. We do not consider His knowledge, power, and authority as ***derived*** from any source. Nothing about God is a result of a *derivative*.

God's ability to cause or create miracles is inherent. A miracle is an event that occurs outside of or beyond the limits or laws of nature. Man cannot perform a miracle. He must operate within the laws of nature. God is not restrained or limited by the laws of nature. He created them. Providential events are akin to miracles, but are within the limits of physical laws. God can and does use providence to control His universe.

Similarly, God's ability to breathe-out inspired Words is inherent. His innate or inherent ability, authority, and power to speak Words given by *"inspiration"* is not transferable to man, just as His innate ability to create or cause a miracle is not transferable to man. *"Inspiration"* is a miracle. Man must operate within the laws of nature. God is beyond the restraint of nature in every way.

God can and does grant *"acquired authority or power"* to certain men such as the Apostles and prophets to perform miracles, but the inherent ability is not transferrable. The inherent ability remains with God who alone has none of the restraints of man's dimensions. The Holy Spirit, who indwelt the Apostles, actually performed the miracles based on the *acquired authority (power)* granted to those 'certain' men (Acts 3:12).

In like fashion, God grants man the authority to translate His Words into the languages of the world. However, the innate power of *"inspiration"* inherent in God is not transferrable to man. Men simply recorded the original inspired Words breathed-out by the innate power of God. The men who recorded the Words were not inspired and did not possess the inherent power of God to inspire Words.

The inspired Words given by an omniscient, omnipotent, and omnipresent God and translated into words chosen by man have **"acquired authority"** or **"acquired power."** The Words do not have the *innate or inherent power or authority* of the original inspired Words given by God. The 'original' Words of God are fixed, permanent, unchanging, inspired, inerrant, infallible, and Preserved by His innate or inherent power. Therefore, we do not call the words chosen to translate the original Words of God inspired, although God grants

acquired authority or power to them, if they are accurate and faithful translations of His Words (see the policeman illustration below). Surely, many people are aware of the diminished power present in dynamic equivalent translations when compared to the dynamic power of formal, verbal equivalent translations.

Translations Are Not Derivatively Inspired

Some people are attributing derivative inspiration to translations. Many people teach that the King James Bible is derivatively inspired. A derivative implies *change*. Synonyms of "derivative" are unoriginal, imitative, plagiaristic, copied, derived, lacking in originality, offshoot, by-product, spin-off, and end-product of something that is changing. The *antonym* of derivative is original. A derivative word in linguistics is a word formed from another word. The word is similar but can and usually does have a significantly different meaning. It is very likely not to be synonymous (e.g. adding a suffix or prefix to a word may change the meaning significantly). In calculus, a derivative is a measurement of how a value **changes** as its inputs **change**.

Since the Words of God are unchanging in their original pure, perfect, inspired *"jots and tittles,"* **no** derivative can be formed. They are the original. Their 'value' or input is not changing from moment to moment or culture to culture. They are fixed. Translating is simply choosing a word among many possibilities in a receptor-language according to syntax that comes closest to the original-language word. It is not a derivative word, which implies change based on changing 'values,' but it is an accurate representation of the **fixed** inspired Word. The best Biblical translation is a verbal, plenary and formal equivalent translation. This kind of translation matches as closely as possible the original, unchanging input, by translating a verb for a verb, a noun for a noun, etc.. The input is the **fixed** *"foundation,"* the Words of God. This *"foundation"* is more reliable and fixed than the foundation of the largest skyscraper in the world. God's Words are fixed by an eternal, immutable, invisible, God and His immutable promises (1 Tim. 1:17, Heb. 6:18, 8:6, 13:8, 1 Pe. 1:4, 2 Pe. 3:9, 1 Jn. 2:25).

A derivative translation would be akin to a dynamic equivalent translation(s), which changes over time to suit evolving cultures and words. It would be more appropriate to call translations such as the NIV, NLT, and others based upon dynamic equivalent translating, derivative translating. This is suggestive of a changing foundation. In fact, this is true. The corrupted foundation of the new versions changes frequently. This is the reason for the numerous editions of the United Bible Society Texts (UBS) and Nestle/Aland Texts (NA^{28}) Imagine a changing skyscraper foundation. Eventually, the entire building would fall as a result. Is this why the dynamic equivalent translations adopted by many churches around the world demonstrate "falling" doctrine, "falling" faithfulness, "falling" morals, and many other "falling" things?

A derivative is a function that **changes** from moment to moment because it is dependent upon variables. There is no variableness, nor waxing, nor waning with God or His Words (Heb. 13:8, Jam. 1:17). God and His Words are unchangeable. If we claim any translation has derivative inspiration and purity, we are essentially giving those who produce translations every six months in English and frequently in other languages the tacit approval to continue to produce changing 'derivatives' every six months. They may also assume the right to claim their 'new' derivative translation is inspired and pure, which many are presently doing. Where will it stop? Besides, it is a misnomer to claim derivative inspiration for a translation, because the input, which is the original Words in Hebrew, Aramaic, and Greek from God, is fixed. These misunderstandings of inspiration, derivative inspiration, inherent, inherited, innate, and acquired are causing monstrous problems.

For example, the following quotes are from men who are incorrectly claiming derivative inspiration of translations. One author, Dr. Cassidy, said:

> "The year before I had presented a paper that dealt with the doctrine of derivative inspiration. I believe translations are inspired in the derivative sense. That is, the history of the translation is inspired history, the promises are inspired promises, and the prophecy is inspired prophecy. In the plenary sense a bible translation can be said to be inspired, but not in the verbal sense. That has been the orthodox position for several centuries, possibly for a couple of millennia."[73]

Where he goes astray is assigning inspiration to history, promises, and prophecy. This is very similar to the claim that God left us a message and not specific, precise Words. God breathed the **Words.** They are the original Hebrew, Aramaic, and Greek inspired Words. They were given *"once"* (Jude 1:3). He did not inspire history, providence, promises, or prophecy. Furthermore, this author cannot find any proof that derivative inspiration has been an **orthodox** position for several centuries or is from ancient times. Another website maintained by "Baptistpillars" has another article by the same author,

---

[73] This quote was found in this article by Dr. D. A. Waite, Th.D., Ph.D., "Dr. Waite's Reply to Dr. Cassidy" but is NOT Dr. Waite's words. (http://www.deanburgonsociety.org/DBS_Society/waite_reply.htm) accessed 11/01/07.

which discusses derivative inspiration. Again, no documentation of "historical" orthodox support for a "derived" text could be found.

Other authors make similar statements about inspiration. **They are good brothers**, but perhaps they have not thought through their claims or they are attempting to be mediators and 'to soothe ruffled feathers.' We agree that accurate and faithful translations carry imputed or acquired authority (q.v.), but they are not inspired by imputation. *"Inspiration"* is a very special process and results in a specific product of God, which cannot be transferred and cannot be applied to man's productions. Dr. Ken Matto said:

> "Since the King James Bible is based on these pure manuscripts, this authority is imputed to the KJV and is evident because people are still getting saved and lives are changed through the teaching and preaching of the King James Bible...God's Word is preserved for us in the King James Bible and although not inspired as the original autographs were, they carry the authority of the original autographs. **We can also refer to it as "imputed or derivative inspiration"** since the King James Bible carries as much authority as the original manuscripts did. Let me repeat, the difference between preservation and inspiration is, inspiration was when God penned the original manuscripts through the holy men of old and preservation is the keeping of those manuscripts down through time. I hope this clears up the misconception of an "Inspired Translation." The King James Bible is a guided translation of the manuscripts handed down to us which had its birth in the original manuscripts which God gave with appended Divine authority."[74]

---

[74] Dr. Ken Matto, "Is the King James Bible Inspired?" (http://www.scionofzion.com/kjvinsp.htm) accessed 11/01/07.

Conferred Authority or Inspiration?

There is **no** comparison of **imputed** authority to alleged derivative, double, or imputed *"inspiration." "Inspiration"* is a theological and Biblical technical term. God cannot impute the ability to inspire Words any more than He can impute the innate or inherent ability to perform miracles. Similarly, imputed righteousness resulting from faith in the completed work of Christ on the Cross of Calvary does not cause righteousness to be innate in man. It is conferred righteousness. Similarly, authority is conferred upon a representative by a superior authority, but **not** inherent *"inspiration,"* an ability possessed by God only, or the innate ability to perform miracles. Again, *"inspiration"* refers solely to the original and Preserved God-breathed Words *"once delivered,"* which were recorded by the prophets and Apostles.

An Example

For example, a policeman has authority **conferred** upon him by the laws of a society to hold up his hand and stop a speeding eighteen-wheeler, but he does not have sufficient innate or inherent power or strength to stop the vehicle. Similarly, authority is conferred upon an accurate, faithful, verbal, formal translation, but it is not "inspired." *"Inspiration"* is a specific Biblical process that produced a specific product. Similarly, the power, muscle, strength, or ability to perform miracles rested with God; it could not be transferred to the prophets or Apostles, but they were granted **conferred** power or authority **at times**. Without **reliance** on conferred or imputed authority, the policeman mentioned above or the Apostles and prophets would have no power. In other words, power can be (1) authority conferred upon others or (2) inherent power such as that authority and power possessed by God. Similarly, the ability to cause *"inspiration"* of Words was **not** conferred upon the Apostles and prophets nor is it conferred upon translators. *"Inspiration"* is a miraculous process possessed by God, only. Many men claim the men who recorded the Words were inspired. The recorders of the inspired Words of God were not inspired themselves. God did not breathe-out men who then recorded inspired Words. They were simply the agents God chose to record the Words; that is, their *"tongue is the pen of a ready writer."* The men were **not** inspired. In other words, they could not speak original inspired Words nor have the inherent power to speak or write inspired Words. Only God has that kind of power and ability. Paul said:

> *"Which things also we speak, not in the **words** which man's wisdom teacheth, but which the Holy Ghost teacheth; comparing spiritual things with spiritual"* (1 Corinthians 2:13).

The King James Bible is Not Inspired

Every person holding the view that the King James Bible is doubly inspired, derivatively inspired, or derivatively perfect as defined in this work, is not only linguistically and historically incorrect, he is theologically incorrect. The King James Bible is plenarily complete and if that is what a person means by perfect, then that is just fine. In addition, the authority of the King James Bible is **conferred** upon it by the inherent power of a Holy God, who commanded translations (Rom. 16:25-27, 1 Cor. 14:21). Therefore, the King James Bible has **acquired** power, because of the **inherent** power behind it. Its power is evident from the obvious blessing by God of the King James Bible through the changed lives of people and the revivals it has instigated.

No modern 'bible' based on corrupted texts has ever started a national revival. This is similar to the authority of the Apostles to perform miracles. Lives were changed; bodies were healed; people were brought back to life; other similar events occurred, all because God **conferred** authority and power; not because of inherent or innate power and authority of men. The Apostles and prophets were representatives of God, similar to a "representative" policeman of the laws of a community. The King James Bible is a "representative" of God's inspired Words.

An Example

To someone witnessing the birth of a child, while it may erroneously be called a miracle, it is not because it occurs according to the laws of nature that God has established. The birth would be a providential occurrence according to the laws of nature. Certainly, any birth is amazing, but it is not a miracle. A miracle describes a process and product outside the realm of natural laws or human ability. Similarly, man should not look upon the process and product of a translation as a miracle. The miraculous process and product of "inspiration" is the *"once delivered"* Words that form the basis (*"foundation"*) of our doctrine, practice of faith, and translations.

Calling a Translation Inspired Causes Confusion

Calling a translation "inspired" causes students of the Words of God to become confused. It is simply adding to the widespread and growing confusion facing churches in these last days. Certainly, many people have been seeking new ideas or other ways to exalt the glory of the Words of God and the **conferred** authority of accurate and faithful translations, but there has been a "muddying of the water." It almost seems some twisted way of exalting the ability of men and their work and words rather than the glory of God and His Words *"given by inspiration."* Saints repeatedly hearing that translations are inspired will eventually "take their eye off the "ball" (see the "Preface" to this work.).

It is hoped that men would drop their use of the word inspired to refer to any translation because of the tremendous confusion that is generated by these claims. The claims cannot be supported by a careful examination of the Biblical meaning of the word *"inspiration"* in the Bible, which should be our final authority, not some 'scholar,' pastor, missionary, or teacher.

Furthermore, great scorn is generated around the world by the false claims of inspiration for the English King James Bible only. Lastly, the incorrect application of these terms is transferring God's innate power and character to man. In effect, it is transferring God's glory to man by claiming man's translations are equivalent to the God-breathed (inspired) Words *"once delivered."* God help those who have consciously contributed to this confusion among God's people in these last days. Those who have participated in innocence need to change directions.

Proper Use of Inspiration and Authority Will Generate Student Interest in the Original-Language Words of the Bible

Hopefully, proper definitions and application of the words will once again motivate more students to at least study the original languages of Hebrew, Aramaic, and Greek. This desire has been lost over the last several centuries. Now, a plumber, electrician, fireman, construction worker, doctor, lawyer, etc., who has no training at all in the original languages and who desires to "preach," takes his place in the pulpit and begins to proclaim his improper exegesis that is based upon his thoughts and emotions. They have far too often gone awry. This does not mean a pastor/teacher has to be an expert linguist, but he should at least have the tools to use Hebrew and Greek lexicons and dictionaries such as knowing the Hebrew and Greek alphabet. We remember Paul's commandment to Timothy, his son in the faith:

> *"Thou therefore, my son, be strong in the grace that is in Christ Jesus. And the things that thou hast heard of me among many witnesses, the same commit thou to* **faithful** *men,* **who shall be able to teach others** *also" (2 Timothy 2:1-2).*

Paul said, *"that thou hast heard of me."* He spoke Koiné Greek, which was the common-language of the Roman Empire while Latin was the trade-language. These verses (2 Tim. 2:1-2) are a strong statement that relates to the proper training of men who would desire to be teachers because *"they...must give account"*:

> *"...they watch for your souls, as* **they that must give account**, *that they may do it with joy, and not with grief: for that is unprofitable for you" (Hebrews 13:17).*

"It is quite marvelous in how many different ways different classes of professing Christians have contrived to nullify the value of their admission the Bible is inspired. Some would distinguish the inspiration of the Historical Book from that of those which we call prophetical. Others profess to lay their finger on what are *the proper subjects* of Inspiration, and what are not. Some are for a general superintending guidance which yet did not effectually guide; while others represent the sacred Writers as subject, in what they delivered, to the condition of knowledge in the age where their lot was cast. The view of Inspiration which Scripture itself gives us, —namely, that God *is therein speaking by human lips*; so that 'holy men of God' delivered themselves as they were 'impelled,' 'borne along,' or 'lifted up,' (pheromenoi) *by the Holy Ghost*; —this plain account of the matter, I say, which converts 'all Scripture' into something *'breathed into by God,'* (theopneustos) —men are singularly slow to acknowledge. The methods which they have devised in order to escape from so plain a revealed Truth, are 'Legion.' (from *Inspiration and Interpretation* by Dean John William Burgon, pp. 183-184; HDW, my emphasis).

CONCLUSION

One conclusion this author has made and now realizes: "The multiple "opinions", "positions", "views" and similar in the literature concerning *"inspiration"* are related to theologians trying to explain *"inspiration"* as a human process because man was involved in **the process** when in fact the process and product (His recorded Words), are **A MIRACLE** *"once delivered."*

I now believe that this is the great failure of many views. It would be similar to a physician (as opposed to a theologian) trying to explain the virgin birth, or the resurrection, or the raising of Lazarus from the dead etc. in human terms or abilities. It cannot be done. *"Inspiration"* (the process and product) has to be received by faith as a miracle just like other Biblical miracles.

One thing for certain, the Words we have received and their *"inspiration,"* infallibility and inerrancy are a miracle. No human(s) could ever write such a book (the canon of Scripture).

God is the author of the Bible, Jesus the subject of the Bible, and the Holy Spirit, the preserver. Make no mistake; it is "all of God."

Amen.

"But does not St. Paul himself in a certain place express a doubt—saying "I think that I have the Spirit of God? and does he not contrast his own sayings with the Divine sayings, ("not I but the Lord") clearly implying that his own were not Divine? And does he not say that he delivers certain things "by permission, and not of commandment," whereby he seems to insinuate a gradation of authority in what he delivers?—NO. Not one of these things does he do." (from *Inspiration and Interpretation* by Dean John William Burgon, 1861, pp. 54-55 available from The Dean Burgon Society Press or Amazon by typing in the title of the book).

INDEX

miracle, 11, 19, 20, 25, 27, 41,
70, 93, 109, 110, 117, 121
miraculous, 11, 12, 15, 26, 29,
35, 41, 52, 56, 65, 93, 94,
116, 117
misunderstanding, 23, 91
Morris, 16
moved, 10, 12, 17, 27, 28, 33,
34, 35, 43, 44, 59, 68, 89,
93, 96
MS, 9, 102
MS B, 102
MSS, 9, 10, 72, 75, 76, 79, 80,
102
Murdock, 42
Mystical, 25
myth, 47, 66
NASB, 9, 33
Natural Inspiration, 25
Neologian, 78
Neoorthodox, 26
Nestle/Aland Texts, 112
neuter, 94
Niebuhr, 63
ninety-nine, 76, 80
NIV, 9, 33, 112
NLT, 9, 33, 112
old man, 64, 87
Origen, 86
orthography, 11, 53
ou me, 95
paraphrase, 9, 38
Partial Inspiration, 26
participle, 14
pasa, 32, 37, 38
Pauck, 63
Pentecost, 43
perfect, 11, 12, 13, 14, 18, 28,
32, 36, 41, 42, 47, 49, 52, 53,
54, 55, 56, 58, 64, 65, 66, 67,
68, 69, 72, 73, 83, 84, 86,
88, 89, 90, 91, 92, 93, 94,
95, 96, 98, 99, 100, 101, 106,
107, 111, 116

perfection, 12, 18, 52, 53, 56,
66, 67, 68, 83, 86, 99, 100,
101, 106
Peshetta, 42
phero, 34, 120
philosophy, 66, 85, 86, 87, 98
Plato, 85, 86
plenary, 9, 11, 13, 14, 15, 35, 36,
39, 53, 57, 59, 62, 73, 91, 93,
98, 111, 113
policeman, 111, 115, 117
Polycarp, 63, 88
positions, 23, 51, 69, 83, 101,
107, 121
post-Apostolic, 36, 51, 76
postmodern, 48
predicate adjective, 33
Presbyterian, 60, 63
Princeton, 59, 60, 63
printing mistake, 56
process, 11, 15, 18, 19, 20, 25,
26, 29, 33, 35, 41, 43, 45, 52,
56, 65, 86, 91, 93, 94, 101,
102, 114, 115, 117, 121
product, 11, 19, 20, 25, 26, 28,
41, 42, 43, 45, 52, 59, 62, 94,
106, 109, 111, 114, 115, 117,
121
providential(ly), 11, 13, 41, 70,
117
purpose, 23, 26, 52, 98
reasoning of men, 86, 100
reflect, 85, 87, 88, 99, 101
representatives, 90, 117
Robinson and Pierpont, 102
rod of iron, 80
Ruckman, 103, 104
rules of grammar, 14, 55
Ryrie, 25, 36
Schaff, 60
scribal, 10
Semler, 86
Septuagint, 38
Sinaiticus, 76

ABOUT THE AUTHOR

Dr. Williams was born in Ft. Pierce, Florida. He was saved at the age of fourteen at his local Baptist church under Pastor J. R. White where he was active in the church youth group. His local church ordained him to preach the gospel. After graduating with honors from high school, he attended Stetson University where he met his wife, Patricia, and they were married in 1961. Starting in the ministerial program at Stetson and switching to pre-med in his junior year, he graduated with honors with a B.A. After Stetson, he taught high school at Eau Gallie, Florida for two years, and then continued his training at the University of Miami Medical School where he graduated with honors. Following his medical training, Dr. Williams and Patricia settled in New Port Richey, Florida where he practiced Family Medicine as a board certified family practitioner. He was active in his community as a hospital board member for twenty years, a chief-of-staff, president of the medical society, an advisory board member and president of Moody Bible Institute's Florida program, a board member of the Health Planning Commission, and a teacher at his local Baptist church. He helped develop and administrate a multi-specialist medical clinic with forty thousand patients and seventeen doctors. His Biblical training was obtained at Stetson University, Moody Bible Institute, and Louisiana Baptist University. After retirement, Dr. Williams has continued serving the Lord Jesus Christ as an associate pastor, a teacher, and as vice-president and representative for the Dean Burgon Society. He received a Ph.D. in Biblical studies from Louisiana Baptist University. He has traveled to many foreign lands where he has represented the Dean Burgon Society, teaching pastors and participating in evangelistic events. He is author of the several books, *The Lie That Changed The Modern World; Word-For-Word Translating of the Received Texts, Verbal Plenary Translating; Hearing the Voice of God; The Septuagint is a Paraphrase; The Pure Words of God; The Attack on the Canon of Scripture, Origin of the Critical Text,* and *Wycliffe Controversies* in addition to many articles and booklets. Dr. Williams and his wife, Patricia have two sons, five grandchildren, and two great-grandchildren.

BOOKS BY DR. WILLIAMS

WORD-FOR-WORD TRANSLATING OF THE RECEIVED TEXT, VERBAL PLENARY TRANSLATING:

This 270 page perfect bound book may be purchased through www.BibleForToday.org or Amazon.com. There is a vital need for a book to inform sincere Bible-believing Christians about the proper techniques of translating the WORDS of God into the receptor languages of the world. No book like this one has ever been written. It is a unique and much-needed book. The very first requirement for any translation of the Bible is to have the proper WORDS of Hebrew, Aramaic, and Greek from which to translate. It is the contention of this book that the original verbally and plenarily inspired Hebrew, Aramaic, and Greek WORDS have been verbally and plenarily preserved in accordance with God's promises. These preserved WORDS are those received-text-WORDS which underlie the King James Bible. This volume emphasizes the requirement of a proper technique to be used in all translations of God's WORDS. It must be done in a verbally and plenarily translation technique. That is, the Hebrew, Aramaic, and Greek WORDS must be conveyed into the receptor languages, not merely the ideas, concepts, thoughts, or message. This technique is absent in all of the other manuals on Bible translation. Dr. Williams is not the usual sort of writer. He combines the meticulous skill of a Doctor of Medicine with the artistry and acumen of a Doctor of Philosophy to produce this grand volume. May translators and sincere Christians of all persuasions and professions use this important book worldwide! Amazon.com (type in book title) or The Bible For Today Press, BFT #3302 ISBN 1-56848-056-3, Order by PHONE: 1-800-JOHN 10:9, Order by FAX: 856-854-2464, Order by MAIL: Bible For Today, 900 Park Avenue, Collingswood, NJ 08108"

THE ATTACK ON THE CANON OF SCRIPTURE, A POLEMIC AGAINST MODERN SCHOLARSHIP

This 172 page perfect bound book was released in January, 2008. ISBN 978-0-9801689-0-7. This book demonstrates the newest attack on the Words and books of the Bible by modern day scholarship. The changing methods for assaulting the Scriptures are important for those who are concerned about the relentless attempt to destroy them. In a remarkable polemic against modern scholarship, Dr. Williams outlines the most recent means many are using to undermine confidence in the Words of God received through the priesthood of believers. It is available at Amazon.com. (type in book title) or at BibleForToday.org, BFT # 3345.

THE LIE THAT CHANGED THE MODERN WORLD

This book is in hardback from BFT and perfect bound from Amazon, 440 pages in all. ISBN 1-56848-042-3. It is a factual defense not only of the King James Bible, but also of the Hebrew and Greek Words that underlie the King James Bible. The author is a medical doctor, now retired, who has researched this important topic thoroughly. May the Lord Jesus Christ use and honor this study in the days, weeks, months, and years ahead until our Lord Jesus Christ returns. It should be in every layman's library, every Pastor's library, every church library, every college library, every university library, and in every theological seminary library. It is available through Amazon.com (type in book title) or Bible For Today Press, www.biblefortoday.org, BFT # 3125.

THE PURE WORDS OF GOD

This is a perfect bound 136 page book. ISBN 978-0-9801689-1-4. Dr. Williams' book, *The Pure Words of God,* clarifies the use of the word "pure" when it is used to define the Words of God. Should "pure" be applied to translations, to Traditional/Received Texts, or to critical texts? Once the correct application is explained, Dr. Williams clarifies God's commands to receive and keep His pure Words. It is available through Amazon.com (type in book title) or Bible For Today Press at www.biblefortoday.org, BFT #3344.

WYCLIFFE CONTROVERSIES

This 311 page perfect bound book is about Dr. John de Wycliffe (1324?-1384). He is an important person in the history of the Bible and Bible Translating. This book is an attempt to recognize and place in one book the contradictions and confusion surrounding Wycliffe and his colleagues. For example, are the Wycliffe Bible Versions based upon Old Latin Texts close to the received Text or are the closer to Alexandrian Texts that influenced Jerome's Latin Vulgate? In addition, many other questions have been raised in the literature such as who were Wycliffe's close associates who participated in the work; where and when did the Lollards that were associated with him originate; and many other controversies. Dr. Williams provides some evidence for the most likely answers to a number of questions. It is available through Amazon.com (type in book title) or Bible For Today Press at www.biblefortoday.org, BFT #3363.

HEARING THE VOICE OF GOD

This 311 page perfect bound book discusses the critical factors related to the postmodern confusion surrounding this issue. The subject is clearly and realistically approached from a plenary Biblical approach. Mysticism accompanying this issue is refuted. This work investigates the topic as it relates to revelation, conscience, inspiration, illumination, and the voice of the Lord in Scripture. Dr. Williams explains how postmodern philosophy has created an atmosphere that contributes to the confusion surrounding this issue. It is available through Amazon.com (type in book title) or Bible For Today Press at www.biblefortoday.org, BFT #3340.

ORIGIN OF THE CRITICAL TEXT

This 157 page perfect bound book identifies five pivotal points pertaining to the origin of the corrupted Critical Texts that lie behind the modern versions of the Bible. It is important for believers to understand the origin and the influence of these original language texts on doctrine, practice, application, and translation of these false texts. At least one new English version of the Bible has appeared in the market place every six months for the last several decades that is translated from these texts. It is available through Amazon.com by typing in the title of the book or from Bible For Today Press at: www.biblefortoday.org. The BFT number is #3386.

www.ingramcontent.com/pod-product-compliance
Lightning Source LLC
Chambersburg PA
CBHW070834100426
42813CB00003B/617